NUMBERS
Don't Lie

THE BIGGEST NUMBERS IN NEW YORK METS HISTORY

World Championships	Pennants	Playoff Appearances
 2	4	 7

D0877811

Russ Cohen with Adam Raider

TRIUMPH
BOOKS

This book is available in quantity at special discounts for your group or organization. For further information, contact:

Triumph Books LLC
814 North Franklin Street
Chicago, Illinois 60610
(312) 337–0747
www.triumphbooks.com

Printed in U.S.A.

ISBN: 978-1-62937-084-2

Design by Andy Hansen

Photos courtesy of Getty Images except where otherwise noted.

This book is dedicated to die-hard Mets fans everywhere, and anybody who ever took me to a Mets game.

Contents

Foreword

I was very fortunate to win two championships in my career. The first one, in Detroit, happened so quickly. We were such a good team right away, but I was just a part-time player with that group. It was 1984, my first full season in the majors. I played a lot but I also watched a lot. I watched how the older guys prepared to play every night and learned about what it takes to build a winning team and have a winning locker room. That experience would serve me well after I got traded to the New York Mets.

Although I was sad to leave Detroit, I was excited to go to New York because I could tell right away that the Mets were on the cusp of being a contender. I saw some of the same ingredients in that club that I'd seen on the Tigers. Also, I was always a National League fan growing up in Florida. The Phillies were our spring training team and I always listened to Phillies games on the radio.

Gary Carter and I were traded to the Mets within a few days of each other. It was a new city and a new team for both of us so we shared a little bond over that. Gary was one of those guys who was always vocal and very supportive of the other people on the team. He was so excited about playing the game and about having the chance to win a championship. It was later in his career, so I think he really appreciated being on the Mets.

Our manager, Davey Johnson, did a great job of getting all of us our at-bats. I played a lot of shortstop that year, as did Kevin Mitchell and Rafael Santana. I also played some games at third. The important thing was that I was playing. I was good with it. Everyone had a role. Again, I learned early on that it takes everybody pulling together to win.

I didn't party a lot. I was very serious about playing the game. I wanted to be as good a player as I could be and I just never felt like drinking and carrying on too much was the way to go about it. I didn't see anybody on the Tigers doing that and I didn't think that was the way to be with the Mets. But I always got along with everybody. I fit in nicely and no one ever made me do anything I didn't want to do. The guys just accepted you for who you were as a person.

There was the time a few of our guys were arrested after getting into a fight at a Houston nightclub. We came into the locker room the next day and Davey filled us in on what had happened. We just made a big joke about it. We put tape on the guys' lockers to make them look like jail cells. We had a good time with it. Things like that brought us closer together.

We also invented the rally cap. There was a group of us—starters and guys on the bench—myself, Mitchell, Santana, Tim Teufel, Danny Heep, and Bobby Ojeda were involved, among others. We invented this thing where we'd do something stupid with our hats. We turned our hats inside out or we'd put gum on the top. We called it our rally cap and we got creative with it. We had all kinds of stuff going on. It was funny.

So much has been said and written about Game 6 of the '86 World Series and the way we came back to beat the Red Sox in the 10th inning. I remember standing in the batter's circle while Mookie Wilson was at the plate facing Bob Stanley. I knew Stanley from my years in the American League and felt pretty comfortable about my chances if I had to face him. I've always thought I would've had a pretty good at-bat and might've been able to get a single off him. But then he threw a wild pitch, allowing Mitchell to score and the game was tied. Once that happened, I knew we'd find a way to win the game.

Then Mookie hit a ground ball up the line. It came toward Bill Buckner and I thought he moved toward the ball very well. But those ground balls, especially at Shea Stadium, could take a tricky hop. The ball took an in-between hop and went right through his legs. He never even got a glove on it. It was unbelievable. It was like I was watching it happen in slow motion. Right then, I knew the series was over.

Because of how he was fielding the ball, kind of back on his heels, Buckner would've had a tough time with that play regardless. Mookie was moving down the line pretty good trying to beat Stanley, who was covering.

Buckner was one of the first guys in the league to wear the high-top Nikes because he had bad ankles. I'd heard that Boston's manager, John McNamara, would sometimes take him out of the game in the late innings if they had the lead and put Dave Stapleton in for defensive purposes. But this time, Buckner lobbied McNamara to stay in the game. He wanted to be on the field for the last out of the World Series. We heard that from some Red Sox people. In light of the way the game ended, I've always thought that was very ironic.

Going into Game 7, we all were really confident. After the way we came back to win Game 6, we knew it was ours from the beginning. And no team that you're playing, being your equal, could feel good about playing us again. Even when we were down 3–0 in the fifth inning, it felt like nothing. We just felt like it was inevitable that we were going to come out on top.

New York City was an unbelievable place to win. It was so early in my career that maybe I didn't really understand the uniqueness of it yet.

My favorite games as a Met were the ones I played in the World Series, obviously. But there were others. One that comes to mind is a game we played in Pittsburgh in June 1988. It was the last year where we beat up the Pirates really, really bad. They'd been neck-and-neck with us the whole season up to that point. We were down by a run in the ninth inning with two outs. I was up against their closer, Jim Gott, with a 1–2 count. He threw me a fastball and I hit a home run high off the glass in right field. A no-doubter. Well, they had a sellout crowd that day and the place went from going crazy to just quiet. We ended up winning the game 8–7 in the 10th. That was a big game for us. I'll never forget that one.

As far as personal statistics go, I'm proud of the fact that I was able to be a 30–30 player. I'd always hit homers in the minor leagues and I always stole bases. In 1986, I had 220 at-bats, hit 10 home runs and had eight stolen bases. I just thought that if I could get a normal amount of at-bats, I'd probably hit 20 home runs, steal 20 bases, and drive in 80 runs. Sure enough, in 1987, I had 554 at-bats and had 36 home runs, 32 stolen bases, and 99 RBI. I thought of myself as a base stealer first, who could also hit for power. I was a line-drive hitter. Home runs were kind of like accidents that would clear the fence. It wasn't like I was trying to hit them out. I think that's the only way you can be a 30–30 guy. You have to have a baserunner's mentality first. You have to value getting on base and trying to make things happen on the base paths.

As you thumb through these pages, just remember that even if numbers don't lie, they never tell the whole story.

—Howard Johnson

Howard Johnson was a two-time All-Star who played nine of his 14 major league seasons with the Mets. He ranks among the club's all-time leaders in games played (1,154), runs (627), doubles (214), home runs (192), RBI (629), walks (556), and stolen bases (202). In 2013, he was named hitting coach for the Seattle Mariners.

Introduction

So, fellow Mets fans, this is a baseball book about numbers. There's one number that I'm very proud to share with you: 26. That's how many consecutive Mets home openers I've attended with my good friend Aaron Cano since 1988. You might say we're a couple of Opening Day fanatics.

The streak *should* have started a year earlier. On an early spring day in 1987, I stood in line outside Shea Stadium for at least four hours in the cold and was only about 50 people away from the ticket window when they announced that Opening Day was sold out. Disappointed, I went home with two tickets for "Opening Day 2," a dumb promotion the Mets had where they tried to make the second home game of the season feel like the first. Weak, but that's all I could get.

Keeping the streak alive hasn't always been easy. There was the time I drove all the way to Queens from Virginia, leaving my wife home sick on the couch (sorry honey!), plus too many other deviations from my regular schedule to mention here. But it's all been worth it because I have a rich databank of memories to draw from including:

April 12, 1988: Expos vs. Mets. Rock Raines with a leadoff single. Straw homers in the second. Mets win 3–0.

April 3, 1989: Dr. K all the way! Gooden strikes out eight Cardinals on the day. Plus, a Hojo to go. Mets win 8–4.

April 9, 1990: Horrible. Wally Backman…*a Pirate?* Seriously? Andy Van Slyke drives in four runs for Pittsburgh. Mets lose 12–3.

April 8, 1991: Another Gooden gem. Seven strikeouts over eight innings as the Mets top the Phillies 2–1. We're happy with the result, of course, but whose idea was it to have Hubie Brooks batting cleanup? Related note: I still chuckle when I think of how much Philadelphia gave up to get Von Hayes.

April 5, 1993: The Mets' first game against the new Colorado Rockies. Gooden pitches a complete-game shutout. David Nied, the Rockies' would-be ace of the future, gets shelled. Mets win 3–0.

April 28, 1995: Mets torch the Cardinals' Allen Watson for seven hits and six runs in a 10–8 New York win. Rico Brogna's game-winning homer elevates him to folk-hero status. We meet the Mets' assistant GM, Gerry Hunsicker, at a season-ticket-holder event. He always pushed Rico hard.

April 1, 1996: Bobby Jones on the mound for a home opener? That's weird. He gives up six earned runs in just three innings of work. Rey Ordonez, in his major league debut, throws out Royce Clayton from his knees! Mets storm back to beat the Cardinals 7–6. John Franco with the save.

April 12, 1999: Rickey Henderson's return. I never cheered for Rickey and I'm not starting today. Bobby Jones homers in the fifth *and* gets the win. Mets 8, Marlins 1.

April 9, 2001: I definitely have my doubts about starting Kevin Appier against the Braves. What happened to Al Leiter? Mike Piazza with *two* homers. Wow. A shaky Armando Benitez gets the save. Mets win 9–4.

April 1, 2002: Leiter stellar for six. Jay Payton hits a home run. Always loved Jay. Mets over Pirates 6–2.

March 31, 2003: Tom Glavine's awful first game as a Met is a 15–2 loss to the Cubs. Corey Patterson homers twice and has *seven* RBI. We are stunned.

April 12, 2004: Steve Trachsel gets the ball against Atlanta, so you know it's going to be a looooong afternoon. Kaz Matsui with a pair of hits. What a signing. The crowd is all over Mike Hampton. The Mets torch him for seven runs. Mets 10, Braves 6.

April 11, 2005: Glavine strikes out six over six innings in an 8–4 win over the Astros that almost—but not quite—redeems him in my eyes. He runs out of gas too early. Andy Pettitte gets booed (once a Yankee, always a Yankee, I guess). Cliff Floyd looking good with two hits, two RBI.

April 9, 2007: Chase Utley and Ryan Howard go deep for the Phillies. Not good. John Maine must've drawn the short straw. But then, Cole Hamels comes out after the sixth! Mets seize the opportunity and score seven runs in the eighth. Is it my imagination, or do they always seem to have great eighth innings on Opening Day? Mets 11, Phillies 5.

April 8, 2008: My last home opener at Shea and they roll out…Oliver Perez? Ugh. Even with Jamie Moyer throwing marshmallows for Philly, Mets lose 5–2. One bright spot: Carlos Delgado homers to deep center-right in the bottom of the second. What a bomb. Too bad the bases were empty.

April 13, 2009: We almost miss this game because the Mets have jacked up the price of Opening Day tickets and I balk at the extra cost. But Aaron comes through with tickets at the last minute, keeping our streak alive. Big Pelf has a rough night for New York, watching as Padres leadoff man Jody Gerut launches a 1–1 changeup into deep right…right toward us! It's the first-ever home run hit at Citi Field. The ball flies over my head (did you see me on ESPN?) and lands right behind me, breaking some guy's finger. I take a picture of his swollen digit. Heath Bell gets the save. Padres 6, Mets 5.

April 5, 2010: Johan Santana. Now that's an Opening Day pitcher. He goes six innings and strikes out five in a 7–1 rout of the Marlins. David Wright with a two-run homer in the first. Jason Bay triples in the sixth. Is it possible I was wrong about this signing? Don't answer that.

April 8, 2011: Jordan Zimmermann is throwing darts for the Nats. There are better days in store for R.A. Dickey. Mets keep it close until the eighth, when the bullpen implodes. So much for my theory about the Mets always having great eighth innings. Nationals 6, Mets 2.

April 5, 2012: Johan pitches five scoreless innings in a 1–0 win over the Braves. Ramon Ramirez gets the win. David Wright with the lone RBI. He has to be the Mets' best-ever Opening Day hitter.

April 1, 2013: The Padres. We can't lose to them again, can we? Jon Niese gets the nod. He's no Tom Seaver, but he'll have to do today. With two outs in the seventh, Colin Cowgill hits a grand slam. Did this really just happen? Mets in a rout, 11–2.

Mets fans are among the most passionate in sports. And now, thanks to me, there are some in Sweden. A friend and fellow sportswriter, Risto Pakarinen, was looking for a baseball team to adopt. I suggested the Mets and he was off and running. He studied the team's history, bought his wife and kids some swag, and insisted that I chaperone him and his family to a game at Citi Field. They actually flew in from Sweden! The first thing they did was take a picture in front of the original Home Run Apple.

Win or lose, Met fans bleed orange and blue.

—Russ Cohen

First Overall Pick Plays

0

Major League Games

In 1976, the Mets came under fire for not outbidding the Yankees for the services of free agent superstar Reggie Jackson. It wasn't the first time they blew an opportunity to get the home run–hitting outfielder. Years earlier, the Mets passed on Jackson to use the first overall pick in the 1966 draft to select Steve Chilcott, a lefty-hitting catcher who would never play baseball in the major leagues.

Jackson, for his part, alleged in his 2013 autobiography *Becoming Mr. October* that he was told the Mets didn't draft him because he was a black man dating a Mexican woman and the team didn't want to deal with the potential backlash. It's not a completely outrageous assertion, given the ultra-conservative state of baseball at the time.

Scouted by Casey Stengel, Chilcott was envisioned by the Mets to be their catcher for the next decade. But first, they dispatched the 17-year-old to the minor leagues, where he played with future Mets like Tug McGraw and Ron Swoboda.

In 1967, Chilcott was leading Winter Haven of the Florida State League in virtually every offensive category—he was also leading the league with 20 doubles—before suffering the freak shoulder injury on July 23 that would eventually derail his baseball career.

> **... he was also leading the league with**
> **20 doubles.**

Chilcott was on first when there was a force at second. He slid into the bag and, believing he'd been called out, got up and started to jog off the field. Once he realized he had actually been called safe, he dove awkwardly back to the base. The infielder fell onto Chilcott's right shoulder—his throwing shoulder. It was never the same.

Over the next three seasons, Chilcott suffered over a dozen semi-dislocations. He often took cortisone shots to reduce inflammation before finally going under the knife to repair the shoulder permanently. Sports medicine wasn't what it is today, and Chilcott never regained his throwing and hitting strength.

Sometime later, he suffered a split kneecap when he fell on a sprinkler head.

Despite a series of heartbreaking setbacks, Chilcott refused to give up his dream of playing major league baseball. Eventually, he was traded to the Yankees, but his injury woes continued. In 1972, a

Steve Chilcott is one of three first overall picks who never played in the majors.

Matt Bush	San Diego Padres	2004
Brien Taylor	New York Yankees	1991
Steve Chilcott	New York Mets	1966

broken right hand in spring training ruined his chances of making the team as Thurman Munson's backup.

It wasn't easy to walk away from baseball, which Chilcott did at age 24. But he used a portion of his signing bonus to invest in real estate, worked as a carpenter, and built a new life for himself in relative anonymity.

Reggie, as is his fashion, took the opposite approach. In his brutally candid memoir, he referenced all the teams he wished he'd played for throughout his career and how much better off those teams would have been with him in the lineup. That included the Mets,

It wasn't easy to walk away from baseball, which Chilcott did at age 24.

who he believed would have won the 1973 World Series with him on their side instead of Oakland's.

"I think about that sometimes," he wrote. "I would've been coming up just as that team was finally improving. They had all those great arms: Tom Seaver, Jerry Koosman, Jon Matlack, Nolan Ryan, Tug McGraw. Oh boy!"

Patient Olerud Bats

.354

In his prime, John Olerud was one of the best line-drive hitters in the game. In 1998, his second year with the Mets, Olerud hit a club-record .354 in 160 games.

Olerud won back-to-back World Series championships with the Blue Jays in 1992 and 1993. Despite putting up solid numbers over the next several years, he failed to replicate the gaudy statistics of his breakout performance in 1993 when he led the league with a .363 batting average, a .473 on-base percentage that was tops in the majors, and career-highs in hits (200), runs (109), home runs (24), doubles (54), and RBI (107).

After the 1996 season, Olerud was battling veteran Joe Carter and up-and-comer Carlos Delgado for a spot at either first base or designated hitter. Delgado was younger and less expensive, making the veteran Olerud expendable. In a deal that set a baseball record for cash changing hands, the Blue Jays traded Olerud to the Mets for pitcher Robert Person and gave the Mets $5 million of the first baseman's $6.5 million salary. Toronto fans are still crying over that one. Person went 8–13 with a 6.18 ERA in two-plus seasons with the Jays.

With the Mets on the hook for just $1.5 million of his salary, Olerud had to be the best bargain in baseball. Coming off a disappointing final season in Toronto where he batted .274, he saw his average jump to .294 with 22 homers and 102 RBI. The Mets went 88–74 and missed the playoffs, but fans were finally excited to come to Shea again after six straight losing seasons.

Olerud was a two-position star (first base and pitcher) at Washington State University. His coach, Bobo Brayton, thought the world of him. "When I made up the lineup," Brayton once said, "I always put Ole in the third spot—where you want your best all-around player—and filled in around him. He led the world in everything."

Olerud had an unusual practice of wearing his batting helmet at all times—even while playing the field. In college, he suffered a brain hemorrhage and an aneurysm during a morning workout. Though he recovered, doctors advised him to wear a protective batting helmet while playing first base or pitching in order to protect against line drives and collisions with baserunners that might result in contact with the skull. That he still wore his helmet as a pro probably had less to do with excessive caution than with habit and superstition.

BIG MAN ON CAMPUS

John Olerud was one of the best all-around college baseball players ever. As a freshman in 1987, he batted .414 and finished 8–2 with a 3.00 ERA on the mound. He exploded as a sophomore, hitting .464 with 21 home runs and 81 RBI while compiling a 15–0 record with a 2.49 ERA, easily winning National Player of the Year. Even while recovering from that scary aneurysm, he hit .359 with five homers and 30 RBI in 78 plate appearances. There's even an award named after him: the John Olerud Two-Way Player of the Year Award, given to the best two-way player of the season. In 2007, John was inducted into the College Baseball Hall of Fame.

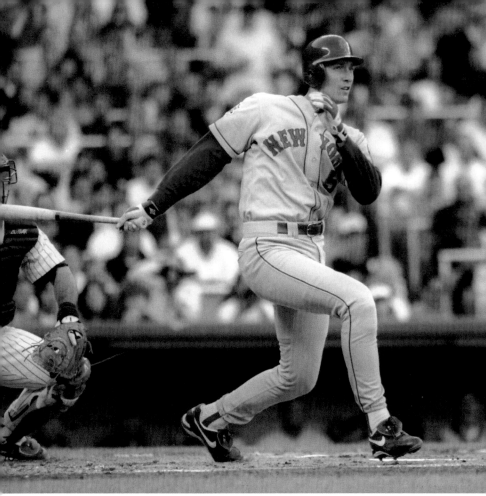

Olerud drives the ball in a June '97 game against the Yankees. *(Linda Cataffo)*

At 6'5", 205 pounds, Olerud reminded some of the Splendid Splinter himself, Ted Williams. Both were tall and lanky lefties with power and a great eye at the plate. Olerud wasn't flashy—he could lull an opponent to sleep by running up pitch counts—but fans really took to him. The Seattle native took to the Big Apple, too. By the end of April 1998, he was hitting a cool .359. A month later, his average was up to .371 and never fell below .339. Thanks to a 23-game hitting streak, he finished the season at .354, a Mets record that stands today. His on-base percentage of .447 is also a team record.

For the second consecutive season, the Mets finished 88–74. Olerud again had 22 home runs and 93 RBI and yet he was only 12th in MVP voting.

In 1999, he also set the team record for most walks (125) and joined Robin Ventura, Edgardo Alfonzo, and Rey Ordonez on the cover of *Sports Illustrated* with a caption reading, "Best Infield Ever?" It might have been. The starting foursome was incredibly efficient, accounting for only 27 errors on the season.

After the Mets fell to Atlanta in the NLCS, Olerud—who hit .296 and led the Mets with two homers and six RBI in the series—became a free agent. Although he enjoyed his time in New York, and at times seemed to be leaning toward staying, the opportunity to return to his native Washington and play for his hometown Mariners proved too hard to resist.

Olerud's time with the Mets might have been brief, but its impact was great.

GREATEST EVER?

They weren't together for very long, but the infield of Olerud, Alfonzo, Ordonez, and Ventura was a joy to watch. Their sharp defensive play is a big reason why New York's pitching staff allowed only 20 unearned runs in 1999, the fewest since 1912 (not counting seasons shortened due to war or labor disputes).

Unearned Runs Allowed

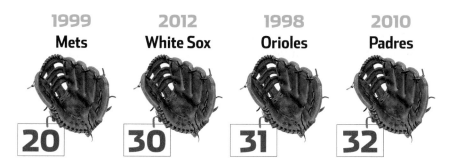

1999	2012	1998	2010
Mets	White Sox	Orioles	Padres
20	30	31	32

Fonzie Bats a Fantastic

.444

Edgardo Alfonzo wasn't named MVP of the 2000 NLCS. That honor went to Mike Hampton. But in batting 8-for-18 with five runs scored and four RBI against St. Louis, "Fonzie" was the Mets' best hitter. His consistency made it easy for his teammates to drive him in. His postseason series average of .444 was the highest in Mets history.

Alfonzo was an undrafted free agent signed out of his native Venezuela in 1991 and he made his major league debut with the Mets four years later. His breakout campaign came in 1997 when he batted .315 with 163 hits in 151 games—the first of nine consecutive seasons with 100 or more hits.

A versatile infielder, Alfonzo spent much of his time in New York moving back and forth between shortstop, second, and third, depending on the organization's needs at any given time. In 1999, the Mets signed free agent third baseman Robin Ventura, prompting Fonzie to shift from third to second.

At second base, his defensive abilities really flourished. In turning 98 double plays and boasting a .993 fielding percentage, he was finally recognized as one of the best defensive players in the game. He took his offense up a notch that season, too, batting .304 with a career-high 27 home runs and 108 RBI. On August 30, he put on one of the great single-game performances ever by a Met, tying a record with six hits (including three homers) in a 17–1 rout of the Houston Astros. In the playoffs, he hit three home runs in the NLDS to help lead the Mets past Arizona.

By now, Alfonzo was really becoming a fan favorite in Queens. He had not only developed into one of the Mets' best all-around players, winning a Silver Slugger award and finishing eighth in National League MVP voting, but he also had a friendliness and approachability that made him seem doubly deserving of all the accolades he was receiving.

In a 2000 season that opened with a 5–3 loss to the Cubs at Japan's Tokyodome, Alfonzo delivered more of the same: 25 home runs, 94 runs batted in, his second consecutive year of 40 or more doubles, and career-bests in batting average (.324) and OPS (.967). Those are eye-popping numbers for a second baseman. He was an All-Star for the only time in his career and the 94–68 Mets had their mojo working for them heading into the playoffs.

His breakout campaign came in 1997 when he batted .315 with 163 hits in 151 games—the first of nine consecutive seasons with 100 or more hits.

The Mets made quick work of the San Francisco Giants and their allegedly chemically enhanced slugger, Barry Bonds, in the NLDS. Superb Giants pitching held the Mets to a paltry team average of .210 in the series, which New York won in four games. Alfonzo led the way batting .278 with a dinger and five RBI.

Next up for the Mets were the dreaded Cardinals. Mark McGwire, another heavy hitter whose reputation was ravaged by baseball's steroid scandal, only pinch-hit in the series because of patellar tendinitis in his knee. St. Louis was facing a Mets team playing its best baseball of the season.

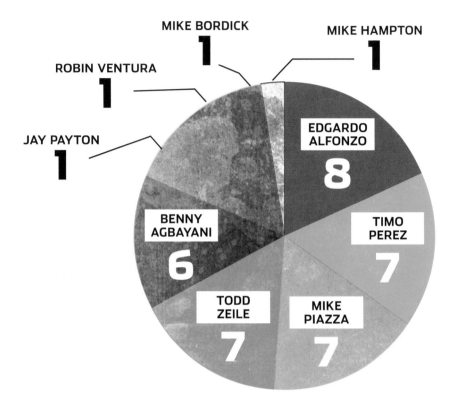

METS HITS IN THE 2000 NLCS

MIKE BORDICK
1

MIKE HAMPTON
1

ROBIN VENTURA
1

JAY PAYTON
1

EDGARDO ALFONZO
8

TIMO PEREZ
7

BENNY AGBAYANI
6

TODD ZEILE
7

MIKE PIAZZA
7

Against the Cards, the Mets scored at least six runs in each of their four victories. Alfonzo, hitting second behind Timo Perez, went 1-for-3 with an RBI in Game 1. The late Darryl Kile pitched a solid seven innings for the Cardinals but Hampton didn't yield an earned run. Alfonzo got two more hits in Game 2, including a triple, and he helped pace the Mets to a 6–5 win behind the arm of Al Leiter. He went 2-for-4 in a Game 3 loss. In Game 4, St. Louis manager Tony La Russa raised some eyebrows by going back to Kile on three days' rest. The move backfired. Kile had nothing left in the tank, blowing a 2–0 lead as the Mets stormed back to win 10–6. Hampton pitched a complete-game shutout and Alfonzo went 2-for-4 as the Mets eliminated the Cardinals in Game 5 to advance to the World Series.

Alfonzo not only batted .444 in the NLCS but also had an OBP of .565, meaning he was on base more than *56 percent* of the time in that series. Mike Piazza hit .412, Todd Zeile hit .368 with eight runs batted in, Robin Ventura had only three hits but knocked in five runs, and Perez crossed home plate eight times.

Like so many Mets of that era, reaching the 2000 World Series was the crowning achievement of Fonzie's career. In eight years with the club, he amassed a career .292/.367/.445 line in 4,449 plate appearances. He left

Alfonzo led the way batting .278 with a dinger and five RBI.

as a free agent in 2002, signing a four-year deal with the Giants worth $26 million. But he never returned to the heights he enjoyed as a Met. He retired in 2006 following a forgettable season split between the Angels and Blue Jays.

In 2014, Alfonzo was named a minor league coach in the Mets' system.

Wally Backman's

.989

Fielding Percentage

Never the fastest or most talented player, Wally Backman became one of the most popular (if underrated) Mets of his era by playing a throwback-style of baseball. In 1985, the scrappy, hard-nosed second baseman set a Mets franchise mark for fielding proficiency.

Selected 16th overall by the Mets in 1977, Backman moved up quickly though quietly through the minor league ranks. Most fans had never heard of him by the time he got his September call-up in 1980. He singled and got an RBI in his first major league at-bat.

In his first few seasons, he was nothing more than a part-time infielder. Playing mostly second base, he also spent some time at shortstop and third base, but didn't really distinguish himself at either position. Even though it was clear that he belonged at second, there always seemed to be others ahead of him on the depth chart, like Gold Glove–winner Doug Flynn, or Brian Giles, a darling of the organization who offered a bit more offense and speed.

Opportunity knocked in 1984 when the Mets left Giles unprotected in the Rule V draft and he was claimed by the Milwaukee Brewers. That seemed to be the break the 24-year-old Backman was waiting for. He appeared in 128 games, batting .280 with 32 stolen bases. He was a spark plug on an up-and-coming team and new skipper Davey Johnson loved him. Johnson had managed Wally in the minors when they won an International League title with the Triple-A Tidewater Tides. Backman had so impressed Johnson that when he became the Mets manager in 1984, he brought Backman with him.

When you think Wally Backman, you think about a player full of piss and vinegar who always made the play in the hole between first and second base. He was the guy whose uniform always looked like it had been dragged through the dirt. With a dive or an outstretched glove, he got the most out of his 5'9", 160-pound frame, and Mets fans adored him for it.

He appeared in 128 games, batting .280 with 32 stolen bases.

In 1985, Backman's only year as a regular, he led NL second basemen (and set a Mets record for that position) with a .989 fielding percentage to go along with 272 putouts and only seven errors. He also turned 76 double plays. At the plate, he was the two-hole hitter in a very potent lineup, churning out a career-high 142 hits and a league-leading 14 sacrifice bunts.

The following season, the Mets were tabbed as a World Series contender. Backman and leadoff hitter Lenny Dykstra were dubbed "the Wild Boys." They were a dynamic 1-2 punch and they had similar styles: balls-to-the-wall baseball. Shortly after the Mets' magical season ended, the team put out a video called *A Season to*

BACKMAN PLAYS THE FIELD

Of **649** chances in 1985...

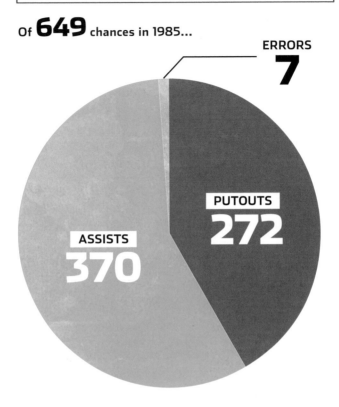

ERRORS
7

PUTOUTS
272

ASSISTS
370

Remember and Duran Duran's hit single "Wild Boys" was featured during the segment on Dykstra and Backman.

Backman didn't have enough at-bats to win a batting title in 1986 but his .320 average was impressive nonetheless. He did head into the 1987 campaign as a regular, but he—and the team—had an off year, and the Mets missed the playoffs.

While the '88 Mets were back to being a contending team, their second baseman was back to being platooned. He managed to hit .303 in a reduced role and tied his career-best fielding percentage of .989. Tim Teufel, New York's other second baseman, was attracting more and more attention as his play improved. After the

Mets lost in the NLCS to the Los Angeles Dodgers, they decided to make some changes.

That December, Backman was traded to the Minnesota Twins for a trio of minor leaguers. He kicked around the league for five more years before hanging up his spikes.

During his playing days, it was easy to envision Wally one day joining the coaching ranks. He eventually became a minor league skipper with the White Sox's Single-A team in 2001. The following year, he led Double-A Birmingham to a Southern League championship. In 2004, he added another championship to his resume with the Diamondbacks' Single-A affiliate. His stock as a major league managerial candidate was rapidly climbing, especially after he was named Minor League Manager of the Year by *The Sporting News*.

He managed to hit .303 in a reduced role and tied his career-best fielding percentage of .989.

After being named manager of the Arizona Diamondbacks, reports surfaced in the press that Backman had an arrest record that included a 2000 drunk driving bust (for which he pleaded guilty) and a 2001 charge for assaulting his wife and one of her friends during a dispute in the family's Oregon home. The Diamondbacks had to admit they hadn't conducted a background check on Backman and decided to fire him after only four days on the job.

In 2010, Backman—who was managing the Mets' Brooklyn Cyclones farm team at the time—interviewed for the vacancy created when the Mets fired Jerry Manuel. He was, at least among many Mets fans, the sentimental favorite. The job eventually went to Terry Collins. Wally was disappointed, but continued working in the minors, biding his time until he gets another chance to manage or coach in the majors.

There's Only

1

David Wright

In a book about important Mets numbers, you won't get very far without seeing the name David Wright. New York's star third baseman makes a compelling case as the best position player the Mets have ever had. Through 2014, he ranked No. 1 on the club's all-time lists in hits (1,702), doubles (375), RBI (939), walks (713), plate appearances (6,531), at-bats (5,707), runs scored (907), extra-base hits (631), total bases (2,819), and sacrifice flies (65).

Wright is as much the face of the Mets as Tom Seaver was in his day. The oft-told story of how that came to be begins in December 1999, when the Mets acquired left-handed pitcher Mike Hampton and outfielder Derek Bell from the Houston Astros for outfielder Roger Cedeno, rookie right-hander Octavio Dotel, and minor league lefty Kyle Kessel. When Hampton signed with the Rockies after one year with the Mets, New York received a compensatory pick, 38th overall, in the 2001 draft. The Mets used it to select Wright, the pride of Hickory Creek High School in Chesapeake, Virginia.

Having grown up a pop fly from Harbor Park, former home of the Mets' Triple-A affiliate, Wright frequently went to see the Norfolk Tides play. In fact, he was playing for the Tides in 2004 when he was called up to make his major league debut in Queens.

Wright was an immediate hit at Shea and finished that first season with 14 homers in just 69 games. The following season, he hit 42 doubles and had 102 RBI.

At 22, he was already being called one of the best third basemen in the game, which,

*Through 2014, Wright ranked **No. 1** on the club's all-time lists in more than 10 categories.*

for a Met, was quite a feat. Before Wright, stability in the hot corner was rare. To date, 153 players have played at least one game at that position since 1962.

"I try to do whatever I can to help the team win," he said. "I am just one ninth of the lineup. I don't try to do more than that and definitely don't try to do less than that. I like to think that I play with some emotion and bring a spark to the lineup. I don't have blazing speed; I have to be a smart base runner. If I pick up on something, and get a good jump, I can steal a few bags here and there."

In 2006, he was an All-Star for the first time and his 116 RBI ranked seventh in the National League. He was a big reason the Mets made it as far as the seventh game of the NLCS. It was, thus far, his only taste of postseason baseball. Unfortunately for Wright, the Mets have had a losing record in all but four of his seasons with the club, prompting many observers to wonder if perhaps Wright's prime years were wasted.

In addition to his career marks, Wright also owns the single-season club record for most total bases (334, set in 2008) and shares the record for RBI in a season, with 124.

DID YOU KNOW? David Wright is the Mets' all-time leader in strikeouts with 1,201. He's also grounded into a club-worst 148 double plays.

DAVID WRIGHT: MILESTONES IN SIGHT

GAMES PLAYED

1,853	1,508	1,322	1,235	1,201
Ed Kranepool	**David Wright**	Bud Harrelson	Jerry Grote	Cleon Jones

HOME RUNS

   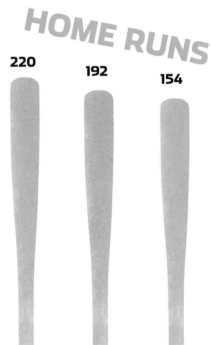

252	230	220	192	154
Darryl Strawberry	**David Wright**	Mike Piazza	Howard Johnson	Dave Kingman

Wright's been almost as valuable in the field as he's been at the plate. He led the National League in putouts as a third baseman in 2009, 2010, and 2012, and assists in 2005, 2008, and 2010. His 34 double plays in 2010 was tops among all NL third basemen. He's a two-time Gold Glove winner (2007 and 2008) who probably should have won a third in 2012, when his 16 defensive runs saved were double that of the player with the next-most, Dodgers third baseman Luis Cruz (who only played 427 innings at the position).

But Wright has been more than just a stat machine. Much more. He's always been a stand-up guy who doesn't duck out the back door of the clubhouse to evade reporters after a tough loss. He's brutally honest about his own play but quick to defend a struggling teammate. He's been a true leader, so much so that in 2013 he was named the fourth captain in the history of the franchise. His tremendous performance for Team USA in the World Baseball Classic that season earned him the nickname "Captain America."

It's hard to imagine that Wright's No. 5 won't one day join No. 41 (Tom Seaver), No. 14 (Gil Hodges), and No. 37 (Casey Stengel) on the left-field fence at Citi Field.

The 2014 season ended with some uncertainty, as Wright was shut down in early September due to an ailing shoulder. The injury played a big part in a career-worst season in which the seven-time All-Star hit just .269 with eight homers and a .698 OPS in 134 games.

1.2

Percent:
The Strawberry Snub

Of all the numbers associated with Darryl Strawberry, including his 335 career home runs, 1,000 RBI, and eight consecutive All-Star appearances, there's one that sums up his epic tumble from superstardom: 1.2. That's the percentage of Hall of Fame ballots on which Strawberry's name appeared in 2005, his first year of eligibility.

To have seen Straw in his prime, when the ball exploded off his bat like a mortar round, one had the sense this kid was destined for greatness. How did a career that began with expectations taller than the New York skyline go so terribly wrong?

Growing up in Los Angeles, Darryl had a front-row seat for the ramifications of addiction. His parents' marriage ended in divorce, a casualty of his father's excessive drinking and gambling. He channeled his energy (and frustrations) into sports, excelling in basketball and baseball. He made Crenshaw High School's varsity baseball team as a sophomore and, with his tall frame and quick swing, drew early comparisons to Ted Williams. Major league scouts soon descended on Crenshaw to check out the phenom who would bat .371 as a junior and .400 as a senior. One scout called Strawberry "the best prospect I've seen in the last 30 years."

There were at least a dozen clubs prepared to use their first choice in the 1980 draft on Strawberry. But thanks to their last-place finish in 1979, only the Mets could make Darryl the first overall pick (Michael Strawberry, Darryl's older brother, was a late-round pick of the Dodgers that same year but never played in the majors).

The power-hitting right fielder was toiling for Triple-A Tidewater when he was called up to make his big league debut on May 6, 1983, as the Mets hosted the Reds. GM Frank Cashen would've preferred to give Strawberry a little more time in the minors for seasoning but New York had lost 15 of its previous 20 and needed a boost in the worst way. Batting third behind Mookie Wilson and

DARRYL STRAWBERRY'S HOME RUNS BY TEAM

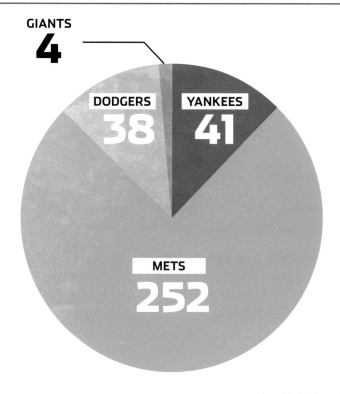

GIANTS
4

DODGERS
38

YANKEES
41

METS
252

Darryl Strawberry acknowledges the crowd after his eighth-inning homer in Game 7 of the 1986 World Series. *(Keith Torrie)*

Tucker Ashford, Strawberry went 0-for-4 with one stolen base in a 7–4 New York win. He went on to play 122 games that year, batting .257 with 26 homers and 74 RBI—good enough to be named the National League Rookie of the Year.

In 1985, Darryl underwent surgery to repair a thumb injury suffered when he made a diving catch. Despite missing 43 games, he hit 29 homers and returned in time to help the Mets make a run for the pennant. On October 1, the Mets arrived in St. Louis three games behind the division-leading Cardinals with only six left to play. The game was scoreless in the top of the 11th inning when Cardinals lefty reliever Ken Dayley threw

He went on to play 122 games that year, batting .257 with 26 homers and 74 RBI.

a 1–1 breaking pitch to Strawberry that the Mets slugger blasted into the Busch Stadium clock behind the bleachers in right-center. Straw's homer, estimated at 440 feet, turned out to be the game-winner and it kept the Mets in the pennant race. However, they were unable to catch the Cardinals and were eliminated on the next-to-last day of the season.

The Mets rolled to 108 victories in 1986, with Strawberry hitting 27 homers and knocking in 93 runs. Though he batted only .217 in the postseason, he hit two homers and had five RBI in the NLCS victory over Houston and homered in the Game 7 win over Boston in the World Series.

The following season, he led the league with 39 homers, hit a career-high .284, and drove in 104 runs. In 1988, he again hit 39 homers, drove in 101 runs, and almost won the National League MVP award, but lost to the Dodgers' Kirk Gibson by a mere 36 votes.

While Strawberry had emerged as one of the game's brightest stars, he'd developed a sometimes contentious relationship with fans, teammates, and managers who felt he was giving less than his best effort (he famously took a swing at Keith Hernandez on team picture day). The relentless scrutiny he faced helped fuel a growing dependence on drugs and alcohol. A 1989 arrest for domestic violence hinted that his personal life was in even worse shape than previously thought.

In 1990, Strawberry became a free agent after he and the Mets couldn't agree on a new contract. He was angry that the team refused to give him more than a four-year deal and looked west to continue his career. On several occasions, he'd hinted that it was his dream to one day play for his hometown Los Angeles Dodgers, and the mutual attraction was confirmed that November when they gave him a five-year deal worth $20.25 million, the second-richest contract in baseball at the time.

... hit a career-high .284 and drove in 104 runs.

Strawberry left New York as the Mets' all-time leader in home runs (252), intentional walks (108), and a host of other offensive records since broken.

In considering Strawberry's Hall of Fame credentials, voting members of the Baseball Writers' Association of America essentially had only half a career to work with. Over his final eight seasons with the Dodgers, Giants, and Yankees, he missed extended periods to undergo treatment for cancer, was slapped with three drug-related suspensions, and was in and out of rehab. The debate over whether Darryl deserved a plaque between Casey Stengel and Don Sutton in Cooperstown seemed trivial compared to the more serious question of whether he would beat his addictions and live to see the age of 50.

Strawberry did eventually get clean, and even opened an addiction recovery center in central Florida. He patched things up with the Mets, too, receiving a hero's welcome on September 28, 2008, when he joined other Mets legends on the field for the closing ceremony for Shea Stadium. Two years later, he was inducted into the Mets Hall of Fame.

Swoboda's

2

Home Runs Trump Carlton's 19 Strikeouts

On September 15, 1969, St. Louis Cardinals ace Steve Carlton set a major league record by striking out 19 Mets at Busch Stadium. But, in an odd twist, the Mets hung on to win the game 4–3, thanks to a pair of two-run homers by outfielder Ron Swoboda.

Carlton, the 24-year-old left-hander, struck out the side in four of the nine innings as he surpassed the record of 18 strikeouts shared by Sandy Koufax, Bob Feller, and Don Wilson. He even fanned Swoboda twice: on his first and third times at bat. But on his second and fourth trips to the plate, the man teammates called "Rocky" blasted home runs into the left-field seats. Each time, the Mets were trailing by one run and had one man on base.

The win put a little more distance between New York and the Chicago Cubs, who were in the midst in an epic free fall out of playoff contention. The Mets improved to 27–7 over its previous

34 games. During that stretch, they overcame Chicago's 9½-game lead in the NL East to soar to the top of the division.

The victory also marked the 20th straight game in which a Mets pitcher did not allow a home run. Gary Gentry recorded three strikeouts and allowed seven hits, three earned runs, and one walk in six innings of work. Tug McGraw (one hit, one walk, three strikeouts) pitched the final three innings and got the win.

It was a bittersweet affair for Carlton, who pitched his way into the baseball record books by fanning half of the 38 batters he faced— Amos Otis accounted for three strikeouts on his own—but also allowed nine hits, including the two home runs by Swoboda, and two walks.

"It was the best stuff I ever had," a dejected Carlton said later. "When I had nine strikeouts, I decided to go all the way. But it cost me the game because I started to challenge every batter."

Swoboda hit only 73 home runs in his nine-year career, all but four of them coming during his time with the Mets. What he lacked in

RON SWOBODA METS TOTALS

Year	Games	At-Bats	Home Runs
1965	135	399	19
1966	112	342	8
1967	134	449	13
1968	132	450	11
1969	109	327	9
1970	115	245	9

quantity he made up for in quality. He had a flair for memorable long balls, as evidenced by the pair he hit off Carlton. He finished with just nine homers that season.

A year earlier, Ron was pictured on the May 6, 1968, cover of *Sports Illustrated* with the caption "Slugger Ron Swoboda." As a rookie in 1965, in only his second major league at-bat, Ron hit a long, pinch-hit home run over the back wall of the bullpen at Shea Stadium. It was the first of a career-high 19 home runs that year, which led the Mets, and was the most home runs by a Mets rookie until Darryl Strawberry drove 26 out of the park in 1983.

*Swoboda hit only **73** **home runs** in his **nine-year career, all but four** **of them coming during his** **time with the Mets.***

Due to manager Gil Hodges' strategy of platooning batters, Swoboda's playing time was greatly reduced and he played only 109 games (with 327 at-bats) during New York's championship season. In fact, the righty-hitting Swoboda did not get a single at-bat in the 1969 NLCS, in which the Mets swept Atlanta in three games, because the Braves started three right-handed pitchers.

Swoboda was back in the lineup for the World Series, batting 6-for-15 (.400) against Baltimore.

2

Years at the Polo Grounds

Before Shea Stadium opened for business, the expansion Mets played their first two seasons at the historic Polo Grounds.

Like Madison Square Garden, there were actually four Polo Grounds, dating back to the 1880s. The first, north of Central Park, was the only one where polo was actually played. The Mets inhabited the fourth version, located beneath Coogan's Bluff at West 155th Street and Eighth Avenue, a stone's throw from the Harlem River Drive.

About 12,500 New Yorkers braved autumn temperatures and an unrelenting drizzle to celebrate the return of National League baseball at the Mets' home opener on April 13, 1962. The crowd was small but boisterous, undeterred by the dreary weather or, for that matter, the final score: a 4–3 Pirates victory.

Built on the ruins of a previous all-wooden Polo Grounds that burned down, the horseshoe-shaped park was notable for its peculiar outfield dimensions. It was short down the lines (no more than 280 feet to left and 259 to right), distant in the alleys (as much as 449 to one bullpen and 455 to the other), and as long as 505 to center field. As a result, some great hitters would drive the ball 400-plus feet to center for an easy out while some mediocre hitters were hitting pop-fly home runs to left and right. Also, the bullpens were in the outfield…and in play!

The Polo Grounds was best known as the longtime home of the New York Giants, who left for sunny California in 1957. This was the stadium where Bobby Thomson hit his "Shot Heard 'Round the World" to win the 1951 pennant and the legendary Willie Mays, who would close out his Hall of Fame career with the Mets, made his spectacular catch of Vic Wertz's fly ball in Game 1 of the 1954 World Series. The Polo Grounds was also home to the Yankees from 1913 to 1922, the Giants football team from 1925 to 1955, and the New York Titans/Jets from 1960 to 1963. It was also the site of many famous boxing matches including the 1923 heavyweight title bout between Jack Dempsey and Luis Firpo, contested in a ring erected in the outfield.

For all those wonderful memories, too few involved the Mets. Their debut 1962 season wasn't simply the worst in club history, it's widely regarded as the worst season by any ballclub, ever. They won 40 games, lost 120, and finished 10th in a 10-team league. They improved by 11 wins in 1963 but again finished dead-last.

By then, maintenance and restoration work had all but ceased on the Polo Grounds, and the old park was practically begging to be put out of its misery. Players disliked the rundown clubhouse and cramped locker room. They couldn't wait to move to Queens.

On April 10, 1964, a week before Shea Stadium opened, a two-ton wrecking ball painted to resemble a baseball—the same one used to demolish Ebbets Field—smashed into a concrete wall of the Polo Grounds, signaling the beginning of the end for one of baseball's most storied parks. The section housing the center-field bleachers and the clubhouses was the first to go, knocked down to make a hole big enough to drive all the trucks and cranes onto the field to finish the job. Every seat and light fixture was safely removed to sell off to collectors, along with anything else of value.

A public housing complex was eventually built on the site: the Polo Ground Towers.

Tom Seaver Wins

3

Cy Young Awards

He was the face of the Mets for a decade. They called him "The Franchise," "Tom Terrific," and "Boy Scout." Tom Seaver was the first homegrown megastar in the history of the team—a great talent and a great competitor who helped transform the Mets from lovable losers into formidable foes. His three National League Cy Young Awards were deserved recognition of his status as the best player at his position.

The Mets finished last in five of their first seven seasons before Seaver arrived (they finished one from the bottom in the other two years). The closest the team had come to a winning record was in 1966, when they finished 29 games below .500. From the day he made his debut as a 22-year-old on April 13, 1967, he lifted the stink of failure that had hovered over the club. In that first game, he struck out eight Pirates. A week and a half later, he threw a 10-inning complete game to beat the Cubs 2–1 at Wrigley.

In 1969, the Mets captured their first World Series championship behind Seaver's powerful right arm. He took home his first Cy Young that year, leading the major leagues in victories with 25, which accounted for exactly one quarter of the Mets' wins.

One year later, Seaver tied a major league record, striking out 19 San Diego Padres including a record 10 consecutive to end the game.

"Tom does everything well," teammate Cleon Jones said. "He's the kind of man you'd want your kids to grow up to be like. Tom's a studious player, devoted to his profession, a loyal cat, trustworthy—everything a Boy Scout's supposed to be. In fact, we call him 'Boy Scout.'"

He was also a fine leader. Hall of Fame outfielder and Mets broadcaster Ralph Kiner recalled that Seaver "was the driving force behind the players, always pushing the team to be better than they were, never letting them settle."

Seaver was an intelligent pitcher who brought great velocity and pinpoint control with him to the mound. Hall of Famer Hank Aaron once said that Seaver was the toughest pitcher he ever faced. And he wasn't alone. In an ESPN poll, Hall of Fame pitchers Bob Gibson, Jim Palmer, Steve Carlton, Don Sutton, and former Mets

MEET CY YOUNG

Denton True Young (1867–1955) was born in Gilmore, Ohio. His nickname, "Cy," was short for "Cyclone," and he dominated the game with his powerful right arm. Pitching for the Red Sox, Young threw the first perfect game of modern times on May 5, 1904, defeating the Detroit Tigers. He won more games (511) than any other pitcher during his 22 years in the major leagues and was elected to the Baseball Hall of Fame in 1937. A year after Young's death in 1955, Major League Baseball established the Cy Young Award to recognize the best pitcher in the major leagues as voted on by members of the Baseball Writers' Association of America. In 1967, the format was changed so that one pitcher from each league would receive the award.

teammate Nolan Ryan all said Seaver was the best pitcher of their generation.

Seaver won his second Cy Young in 1973, when a late-season surge propelled the Mets into the World Series. His 19–10 record wasn't the best in baseball, but his 2.08 ERA and .976 WHIP certainly were.

The 1975 Mets finished only two games over .500 but there was nothing mediocre about the performance of their ace, Seaver. He went 22–9 with a league-leading 243 strikeouts while allowing only 11 home runs over 280.1 innings to win his third Cy Young.

As a Met, Seaver was selected to nine All-Star teams, led the league in strikeouts five times, put together four 20-win seasons,

Jack Lang, secretary-treasurer of the Baseball Writers' Association, hands Tom Seaver his third Cy Young Award in New York on May 7, 1976.
(Photo via AP Images)

CY YOUNG AWARD LEADERS

Roger Clemens

Randy Johnson

Steve Carlton

Greg Maddux

Tom Seaver

Four others tied

threw five one-hitters, and pitched 171 complete games, including 44 shutouts. He probably should have won a fourth Cy Young, in 1971, when he won 20 games, lost 10, and led all pitchers with a career-best 1.76 ERA and 289 strikeouts. But he was narrowly edged out by the Cubs' Ferguson Jenkins, who went 24–13 with a 2.77 ERA.

The Mets knew they'd found someone special when they signed the Fresno, California, native under unusual circumstances.

The Dodgers drafted Seaver in the 10th round in 1965, but balked at the young pitcher's demand for a $70,000 signing bonus. The following year, he signed a contract with the Braves, who had just moved from Milwaukee to Atlanta.

"In 1966 I was in Long Beach, California, with the Cleveland Indians and we were playing the Cubbies," said former Indians second baseman Vern Fuller. "On that day, they were asking me to share a locker with this kid. There were six Hall of Famers: Ernie Banks, Ferguson Jenkins, Ron Santo, Billy Williams, Cubs manager Leo Durocher, and the kid who threw batting practice, Tom Seaver. He was blowing the ball by everybody. Nobody could touch him,

TOM SEAVER: CAREER AT A GLANCE

Games	**656**
Hits allowed	**3,971**
Runs allowed	**1,674**
Innings pitched	**4,783**
Wins	**311**
Losses	**205**
Winning percentage	**.603**
Games started	**647**
ERA	**2.86**
Complete games	**231**
Shutouts	**61**
WHIP	**1.121**
Saves	**1**
Earned runs	**1,521**
Walks allowed	**1,390**
Strikeouts	**3,640**

except Fred Whitfield. Old Fred could hit 'em. Seaver just threw so darn hard."

"In the off-seasons," Fuller said, "I worked in the hotel business and was running a hotel in the Cleveland area. He came into the hotel for some reason and checked in. I wrote him a note about that day in Long Beach and sent up a cheese tray. He came down and told me he did remember and thanked me for sharing a locker with him."

While Seaver was turning heads in spring training, Major League Baseball hired William Eckert as its new commissioner, replacing the retired Ford Frick. Eckert, a former military man with no real background in professional sports, voided Seaver's deal with the Braves, since his college baseball season at the University of Southern California had already started. In turn, the NCAA ruled that since Seaver had signed a professional contract— regardless of the fact that it had been voided by the MLB commissioner—he forfeited his college eligibility. Charles Seaver, Tom's father, threatened to sue the league. Eckert decided that any team willing to match the Braves' $40,000 contract could enter into a lottery for Seaver.

Seaver's 19–10 record wasn't the best in baseball, but his 2.08 ERA and .976 WHIP certainly were.

The Cleveland Indians were interested, along with the Mets and Philadelphia Phillies. All three team names were written on slips of paper and put into a hat. Then Eckert, with Seaver listening in on a long-distance call, reached into the hat and pulled out a piece of paper. The Mets, the worst team in baseball, won the lottery.

Seaver's exit from New York unfolded almost as dramatically as his arrival. After their appearance in the 1973 World Series, the Mets steadily declined. Seaver vented his frustrations about the club's losing ways to chairman M. Donald Grant, who drove the team into the ground with his authoritarian management style and penny-pinching ways. What began as a behind-the-scenes, internal dispute spilled out into the arena of public opinion in June 1977 when *Daily News* columnist Dick Young came down heavily on the side of Grant by portraying Seaver as deceptive, greedy, and jealous of players he believed to be making more money. Young drew condemnation from peers and readers alike for making himself Grant's mouthpiece, especially after it was reported by rival papers that Young's son-in-law worked in the Mets front office. The conflict of interest was obvious to all except the acerbic sportswriter.

Seaver probably should have won a *fourth Cy Young* in 1971.

In the end, it was a column by Young—in which he invoked the names of Tom's wife, Nancy, and Nolan Ryan's wife, Ruth, and claimed that the Seavers were resentful that Ryan was making more money with the California Angels—that enraged Seaver and ultimately forced the June 15 trading-deadline deal that broke thousands of hearts across the metropolitan area. In what has come to be known as the "Midnight Massacre," the Mets traded Seaver to the Cincinnati Reds for pitcher Pat Zachry, utility infielder Doug Flynn, and minor league outfielders Steve Henderson and Dan Norman.

Seaver pitched another nine seasons in the majors. In 1983, he was traded back to the Mets, then on to the Chicago White Sox, where he picked up his 300th win, before finishing his career with the Boston Red Sox.

In 1992, he was inducted into the National Baseball Hall of Fame with the highest vote to date: 425 out of a possible 430 votes, or 98.8 percent. Not even Babe Ruth, Ty Cobb, or Hank Aaron managed that.

Simply terrific.

Not a Typo:
Rey Ordonez Made Only

4

Errors in '99

Rey Ordonez defected from Cuba in 1993 to pursue his dream of playing major league baseball, leaving behind that island nation's oppressive Communist regime but also friends and family.

Ordonez hit U.S. soil in Buffalo, New York, in 1993. Like others without MLB contracts before him, he opted to play for the St. Paul Saints in the Northern League. After that season he signed with the New York Mets and became instant news. He was a flashy fielder and that would always be his best asset.

After three seasons in the minors, the shortstop made his major league debut in 1996. Right off the bat, he wasn't a player who was going to blend in. His first uniform number was a good indication. He was just the second Met to wear 0. Terry McDaniel was the first in 1991.

RATING REY AGAINST THE BEST

Name	Year	Team	Fielding %	Errors
1. Mike Bordick	2002	Orioles	.9982	1
2. Cal Ripken	1990	Orioles	.9956	3
3. Omar Vizquel	2000	Indians	.9954	3
4. Rey Sanchez	2000	Royals	.9941	4
5. Rey Ordonez	1999	Mets	.9938	4
6. Omar Vizquel	2006	Giants	.9933	4

At the age of 25, the La Habana native had a solid rookie season. He hit .257, which was acceptable, playing in 151 games, and even though he made 27 errors, he had 705 chances, the most in his career. He turned 102 double plays to lead the National League. Those numbers placed him fifth in the Rookie of the Year voting.

When the 1997 season began, the papers were talking about that young shortstop for the Yankees, Derek Jeter, and the flashy Ordonez. There was a new manager, former Met Bobby Valentine, and he was focusing on strong fundamental baseball: good fielding, smart hitting, bunting, and good base running. Ordonez fit the bill for most of that. While he only hit .216, he did get 14 bunt singles, something that was an art form, and he only committed 9 errors all season, helping him to his first-ever Gold Glove—the first by a Mets shortstop since Bud Harrelson won the award in 1971.

In 1998, the Mets infield was very good: John Olerud was a tall, lanky scooper who wore a batting helmet; Carlos Baerga was on second, always a solid fielder; a young Edgardo Alfonzo manned third; and Ordonez found his hitting stroke a bit that season, driving in 42 runs. In the field he made 17 errors but he had 685 chances while turning 82 double plays—good for fifth in the league. Baerga could have turned a few more double plays that season but Ordonez won his second-consecutive Gold Glove, becoming the first Mets player since Keith Hernandez to do that.

Ordonez was a run-saver. This became an important statistic to quantify his worth to the team since he wasn't a strong hitter. Fans could see him make amazing throws from the hole with a rocket arm. He also perfected a pop-up slide that gave him much more range than the average shortstop, especially on balls hit between shortstop and third base.

The 1999 season was a special one for Met fans—a season of renewed hope. The previous season saw the team get over the .500 mark and now they added Robin Ventura at third base to offer some punch and superb fielding. By mid-season it was clear that this infield was arguably the best in the history of the franchise and it had the potential to be the best in the history of baseball.

Ordonez was in his prime in '99, and he played a career-high 1,316$\frac{2}{3}$ innings. He was third in the league in double plays, though while Colorado's Neifi Perez and San Francisco's Rich Aurilia turned more, neither did it while committing only four errors. His .994 fielding percentage was a Mets record, and the .989 fielding percentage for the combined infield was the best in the game. In a 2013 article, *ESPN's* Adam Rubin ranked this infield as the third best all time behind the 1976 Reds and 2009 Yankees. Elias Sports Bureau showed that the 1999 Mets only allowed 20 unearned runs, the lowest total since 1912.

The 1999 Mets finished second to the Atlanta Braves with a 97–66 record, and beat the Reds in a one-game playoff. However they lost to the Braves in the NLCS, four games to two. Following the season, Ordonez racked up his third consecutive Gold Glove.

On May 29, 2000, the Mets lost Ordonez to a fractured arm. With other shortstops filling in, they made it to the World Series, only to lose to the crosstown-rival Yankees. He was missed and his career would never be the same.

He never won a Gold Glove again, and in 2003, as a free agent, he signed with the Tampa Bay Devil Rays. He was gone from Tampa the following year, on to Chicago, where he would finish out his career with the Cubs.

In 2013, his life journey came full circle when a change in migration laws allowed him to return to Cuba for the first time since defecting. He got a hero's welcome.

Hometown Hero Baxter Draws

5

Walks

It's very rare that a player gets to play for his hometown team. Rarer still is the local boy who draws five unintentional walks in one game for that same hometown team.

A productive bench player and occasional starter over three Mets seasons, Mike Baxter was one of seven players drafted out of Archbishop Molloy High School in Queens, though he was the first to make it to the bigs. A 2005 fourth round pick of the San Diego Padres, he opted against jumping from high school to the minor leagues and instead chose to enroll at Columbia University in New York. Following Baxter's freshman year, an opportunity to play in the much more competitive Southeastern Conference prompted him to transfer to Vanderbilt.

Baxter got his next big break when he caught the eye of the Padres while playing in the fabled Cape Cod summer league in

Massachusetts. Ironically, and with a foreshadowing of his future, he was playing for the Hyannis Mets at the time. A shortstop throughout high school who played first and third in college, Baxter was a solid infielder whose outfield play was steadily improving. The Padres signed him on the condition that he play in the outfield. He was one of the last players signed from the 2005 draft.

Baxter spent a good chunk of his twenties kicking around the minor leagues, until September 2010, when the Padres called him up for a nine-game stint. He went 1-for-9. Placed on waivers the following July, he was claimed by the Mets.

> *Baxter spent a good chunk of his 20s kicking around the minor leagues.*

Thrilled to be wearing the uniform of the team he cheered for as a kid, Baxter enjoyed plenty of memorable moments in his brief Met career. On August 8, 2011, with friends and family members in attendance, he played his first home game at Citi Field, a 9–8 win over San Diego. On September 28, facing Cincinnati's Edinson Volquez with two outs in the sixth inning, the lefty hitter launched his first major league long ball, helping seal a 3–0 win.

The following season, Baxter preserved Johan Santana's no-hitter against the Cardinals when he caught a scorcher off the bat of Yadier Molina while crashing into the wall in left field. He fell to the ground, clearly in pain, but never lost his grip on the ball. Mets manager Terry Collins and team trainers ran out to make sure he was alright. A few minutes later, Baxter walked off the field under his own power to a standing ovation. He suffered a broken collarbone on the play, however, and would miss almost two months of action.

 DID YOU KNOW?

In 2012, Mike Baxter helped set an unofficial club record by being one of six Mets to get engaged during the same off-season. The others were David Wright, Kirk Nieuwenhuis, Zach Lutz, Reese Havens, and Josh Satin.

In his first game since being activated from the disabled list, Baxter got a big pinch-hit single to center in the top of the 10th inning to help get a win against the San Francisco Giants.

Less than a week later, on August 4, 2012, at San Diego, Baxter staked his own place in the Mets record book. That night, the 27-year-old became the only Met and first player since Florida's Ivan Rodriguez in 2003 to go 0-for-0 with five *unintentional* walks in a game. However, Baxter wasn't the first Met with five base-on-balls in a game; that honor belongs to speedster Vince Coleman, who walked five times in a 16-inning contest on August 10, 1992.

Baxter's on-base percentage increased by 35 points, from .390 to .425.

Teammates teased Baxter about his feat. "Way to swing the bat tonight," they cracked. Amazingly, his on-base percentage increased by 35 points, from .390 to .425, with the five walks accounting for 35.7 percent of his season total.

Baxter was never quite the same after the injury he suffered in the Santana no-hitter. He was batting just .189 in 155 plate appearances in 2013 when the Mets made the difficult decision to put him on waivers. He was picked up by the Dodgers, with whom he hoped to resuscitate a big league career that was fleeting but by no means uneventful.

Keith Hernandez Wins

5

Gold Gloves

Before he struck out with Elaine and tried to rope Jerry into helping him move some furniture, Keith Hernandez was a key member of the powerful Mets teams of the mid-1980s whose stellar defensive play at first base earned the mustached bad boy the National League Gold Glove Award in each of his first five seasons in New York.

Acquired from the St. Louis Cardinals in June 1983 for pitchers Neil Allen and Rick Ownbey, the former National League co-MVP was coming from a World Series winner to a team that won only 65 games and finished sixth in the NL East in 1982.

A career .994 fielder at first, Hernandez is widely regarded as the best defensive first baseman of his generation—maybe of any generation. He was the master of playing a shallow first base to get the lead runner on bunts and of picking balls thrown in the dirt. Hernandez won the NL Gold Glove 11 years in a row from 1978 until 1988.

Because Hernandez played what is considered an offensive position, his contributions were sometimes underappreciated. The best defensive players sometimes don't get to see their handiwork reflected in a box score, but you'd be hard-pressed to find a player who did more than Hernandez to help his team win.

These days, first basemen are known more for hitting big home runs (think Ryan Howard and Miguel Cabrera). But Keith could hit, too. He was an offensive force, in fact—a No. 3 hitter with a lifetime .296 batting average. He batted over .300 in each of his first four seasons with the Mets and reached double digits in home runs five years in a row. A patient hitter, he led the National League with 94 walks in '86.

A patient hitter, Hernandez led the National League with 94 walks in '86.

He played in two seven-game Fall Classics in his career, earning two rings in the process. He drove in eight runs in the last three games in 1982 as the Cardinals defeated the Milwaukee Brewers, and had three RBI in Game 7 of the 1986 Series, including a two-run single in the sixth inning that cut into Boston's 3–0 lead.

As viewers of current Mets broadcasts have learned, Keith has always had a way with words. He pulls no punches, and his blunt style resulted in a number of altercations during his playing days. During spring training in 1989, on the same day that players were to pose for the official team picture, Hernandez and Darryl Strawberry had to be separated by teammates after Hernandez made a comment about Strawberry's contractual squabble with the club.

Hernandez became a free agent following the 1989 season. He played briefly with the Cleveland Indians before retiring.

That a player who makes a strong case, both statistically and anecdotally, for induction into the Baseball Hall of Fame has not yet been summoned to Cooperstown strongly suggests that

The two-part *Seinfeld* episode in which Keith Hernandez guest stars as himself, "The Boyfriend" (1992), ranks as Jerry Seinfeld's favorite. The sitcom ran on NBC from 1989 to 1998.

Hernandez is still plagued by the Major League Baseball cocaine scandal that made headlines in 1985.

The scandal involved a number of then-current and former members of the Pittsburgh Pirates as well as other notable major league players. Hernandez was among those implicated, and he was called before a Pittsburgh grand jury to offer testimony. It came to light that he'd been using cocaine for years, which helped explain why the Cardinals were willing to trade their All-Star first baseman for a pair of relief pitchers. Cards GM/manager Whitey Herzog wanted Hernandez gone.

MLB commissioner Peter Ueberroth found that Hernandez had not only used cocaine but also had been involved in its distribution. He and six other players received season-long suspensions, which were commuted on the condition that they donate 10 percent of their base salaries to drug-abuse programs, submit to random drug testing, and perform 100 hours of drug-related community service.

Yes, Keith made some mistakes in his life—mistakes for which he has accepted responsibility. But for the record, it was Roger McDowell who spit at Kramer and Newman, *not* Keith Hernandez.

Mets Blow

7

Game Lead (and Glavine Surrenders 7)

There are chokes, and then there are *chokes*. The 2007 Mets blew a seven-game lead by losing 12 of their final 17 games of the season, an epic collapse punctuated by Tom Glavine's disastrous final appearance on the mound for New York.

At the plate, the Mets were fourth in the NL in runs and third in on-base percentage. Despite getting just five starts from Pedro Martinez, they had an above-average pitching staff that posted a 4.26 ERA. How did it all go so horribly wrong? In a nutshell: even with one of the more talented rosters in the league, the Mets came up short in clutch situations and had trouble putting bad teams away.

Then, in September, Philadelphia swept a three-game series at Shea Stadium, giving the Phillies wins in the final eight meetings between the teams. That started a slide from which the Mets never

The largest leads held in September by teams that did not finish in first place in their league (or division, 1969 and later), as compiled by the Elias Sports Bureau. Date of largest lead is listed:

Date	Team	Lead
9/12/07	Mets	7 games
9/1/38	Pirates	7 games
9/6/34	Giants	7 games
9/4/95	Angels	6½ games
9/20/64	Phillies	6½ games
9/8/51	Dodgers	6½ games

recovered. They were done in by ineffective starting pitching, a tired and shaky bullpen, sloppy defensive play, and bats that went ice-cold.

And then there was Glavine, the former ace who padded his Hall-of-Fame credentials killing the Mets as a member of the rival Atlanta Braves. He'd signed with New York as a free agent in 2003 and spent the next five seasons frequently falling short of fans' expectations. This was never more true than on September 30, 2007, the last game of the regular season.

The Mets limped into that critical meeting with the Florida Marlins desperately needing a win in order to have any chance of making the playoffs. A win would not only have kept the Mets even with Philadelphia and forced a one-game playoff for the division title, but it would have tied New York with the Colorado Rockies and San Diego Padres for the NL wild-card.

Even the best pitcher can have an off-day but characterizing Glavine's performance as an "off-day" would be an extraordinary understatement. In what was probably the worst start of his career, Glavine allowed seven earned runs on five hits, two walks, and one hit batter in just one third of an inning. The Mets never recovered. Final score: Marlins 8, Mets 1.

Glavine's all-time record with New York dropped to 61–56 with a 3.97 ERA. There were a handful of pleasant moments along the way: his 300th win and playing in the 2004 and 2006 All-Star Games come to mind. But those would've been afterthoughts compared to beating the Marlins. Rescuing a season on life support would have elevated Glavine from has-been to folk hero in Queens overnight. Instead, he imploded about as badly as a pitcher can and dragged the Mets' slim postseason hopes down with him.

"I'm not devastated," he told reporters that day. "I'm disappointed, but devastation is for much greater things in life."

He was right, of course, but fans didn't want perspective from Glavine—they wanted piss and vinegar. They wanted to know that he was as shocked and angry about how the season had ended as they were. That quote was the little nugget atop a dung sundae that fans will be tasting for years to come.

*Glavine's all-time record with New York dropped to **61–56** with a **3.97 ERA**.*

That October, Glavine declined a $13 million player option to return to the Mets and instead accepted a $3 million buyout. He went back to Atlanta where he pitched a handful of games before retiring.

Manager Willie Randolph, who publicly accepted full responsibility for his team's collapse, surprised quite a few people by keeping his job...until the following June, that is, when he was axed in the middle of the night by GM Omar Minaya.

The Phillies went on to win the World Series in 2008. Appearing on WFAN a few months later, Philadelphia pitcher Cole Hamels poured salt on an open wound by calling the Mets "choke artists." Hamels had a point. By squandering a seven-game lead so late in the season, the Mets had elevated choking to an art form.

Delgado Drives in

9

Carlos Delgado was one of the game's best undrafted players. He started out as a catcher with the Toronto Blue Jays, then signed as a free agent with the Florida Marlins. After just one season there, at the age of 34, the New York Mets traded for the slugger on November 24, 2005. They traded emerging slugger Mike Jacobs, pitcher Yusmeiro Petit, third baseman Grant Psomas, and a minor leaguer. The Mets also got $7 million from Florida to help cover the $48 million he was due.

Mets General Manager Omar Minaya was looking for power in the middle of the Mets lineup and he found it in Delgado, who previously hit 369 big league dingers. His first season in New York was productive, with 38 homers, 114 RBI, and a playoff bid. Between the NLDS against the Los Angeles Dodgers and the failed NLCS against the St. Louis Cardinals he hit four bombs, driving in 11. He was always a run producer.

His numbers, and the team, were a bit off in 2007. He hit 24 home runs to go with 87 RBI, and at the age of 35, the whispers had begun. Has he lost his stroke? Is he going to regain his form? He was always a model citizen in New York. Good with his teammates and the press. The fans loved him.

The Mets were playing the Yankees on a June day at Yankee Stadium during their yearly Subway Series. With the game tied 4–4 in the top of the fifth inning, Delgado doubled in two runs to put his team up 6–4.

Then in the top of the sixth, with the Mets ahead 7–4, Delgado blasted a grand slam. The rout was on but it wasn't over.

Of the **15 runs** *the Mets put up that day, Delgado drove in* **9.**

In the top of the eighth, with the Mets up 12–5, Delgado hit a blast to deep right field. His second homer of the game was a three-run shot that put the Mets up 15–5. Of the 15 runs the Mets put up that day, Delgado drove in nine. Nine RBI in a single game remains a Mets record, though not a major league record; that stands at 12 and is held by two different players.

In 2009, a hip injury limited the normally steady first baseman to just 26 games. He did manage to become the first ballplayer to hit a homer in the Pepsi Porch at Citi Field.

Following a few hip surgeries, the Boston Red Sox signed him to a minor league deal in 2010. After suffering a setback with his troublesome hip he retired in 2011 with 473 homers, 1,512 RBI, and a chance at the Hall of Fame someday.

Carlos Delgado hits against the Yankees at Yankee Stadium. *(Jim McIsaac)*

Tom Terrific Strikes Out

10

in a Row, 19 Overall

On April 22, 1970, Tom Seaver set a major league record by fanning 10 batters in a row, 19 overall, in a 2–1 win over the San Diego Padres at Shea Stadium.

Just before the start of the game, Seaver was handed his 1969 Cy Young Award—the first of three he'd win in his Hall of Fame career.

As dominating an outing as the 25-year-old ace had that day, it should be noted that Seaver wasn't facing the 1927 "Murderer's Row" Yankees. The second-year Padres did have a dangerous slugger in the late, great Nate Colbert and the streaky Cito Gaston to worry about but an otherwise weak lineup didn't put a scare into most pitchers.

"Actually," Seaver's catcher, Jerry Grote, told reporters later, "[Tom] wasn't that strong in the early innings. He just kept building up as the game went on. The cool weather helped and by the end of the game, he was stronger than ever."

After he struck out Al Ferrara to close the sixth inning, Seaver was unhittable. Nine more strikeouts followed, including Ferrara again in the ninth. Mets shortstop Bud Harrelson, who didn't have a single ball hit to him all day, joked that he could've played the game without a glove.

"[Seaver] was fantastic, outstanding," marveled Johnny Podres, San Diego's minor league pitching instructor, who watched the game from his seat by the dugout. "There was no doubt in my mind he'd break that record. He had perfect rhythm and I don't think he'll ever throw that hard again. It's amazing—as hard as he was throwing, he was still hitting the spots. If you didn't swing, it still was a strike."

*Seaver's **136 pitches** included 81 fastballs, 34 sliders, 19 curveballs, and two changeups.*

Seaver's 136 pitches included 81 fastballs, 34 sliders, 19 curveballs, and two changeups. Along the way, he surrendered only two hits, retired the last 16 batters he faced, notched his 13th consecutive regular season victory, and topped the previous club record for strikeouts in a game—which had been 15, set just a week earlier by Nolan Ryan.

As well, Seaver's 19 total strikeouts (in nine innings) tied a major league record set a year earlier by the Cardinals' Steve Carlton in a 4–3 loss to the Mets. Boston's Roger Clemens set a new single-game mark in 1986 with 20 strikeouts and repeated the feat in

A DAY OF FIRSTS FOR SEAVER

FIRST major leaguer to strike out 19 batters in the daytime

FIRST major leaguer to strike out more than eight batters in succession

FIRST major leaguer to pitch a two-hitter on Earth Day

1996. Kerry Wood matched it as a rookie in 1998, pitching for the Chicago Cubs. The record for most strikeouts in an extra-inning game belongs to the Washington Senators' Tom Cheney, who recorded 21 Ks over 16 innings on September 12, 1962.

Seaver's bravura performance on that April afternoon in 1970 overshadowed a fine start by San Diego's rookie right-hander Mike

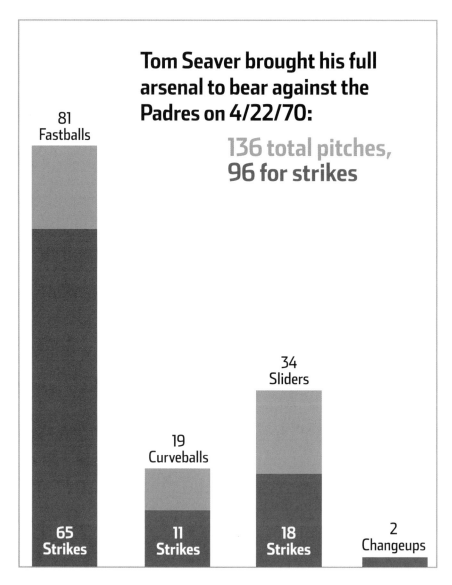

Tom Seaver brought his full arsenal to bear against the Padres on 4/22/70:

136 total pitches, 96 for strikes

81
Fastballs

65
Strikes

19
Curveballs

11
Strikes

34
Sliders

18
Strikes

2
Changeups

While Tom Seaver was making history on the mound against San Diego, Jerry Grote was doing it behind the plate. Thanks to all the strikeouts and one foul pop fly, Grote set a new single-game major league record for catchers with 20 putouts. The previous record of 19 had been shared by John Roseboro of Los Angeles and Detroit's Bill Freehan. Grote, considered one of the best defensive catchers of his day, went on to lead the National League in putouts in 1970 and 1971.

Corkins, who went a solid seven innings and yielded just two runs and four hits in the loss.

New York got on the board in the bottom of the first when second baseman Ken Boswell hit an RBI double to left field. The Padres tied it the next inning on a Ferrara home run. In the bottom of the third, Harrelson put the Mets ahead for good when he tripled to right, allowing Tommie Agee to score.

Seaver was pleased with the result of the game but certainly not doing cartwheels over beating a weak team that would finish with a record of 63–99. Besides, he still had his sights set on a more elusive feat: a perfect game.

Seaver went on to set a new club record for starts in a season with 36, lead the National League with a 2.82 ERA and 283 strikeouts, and appear in his fourth consecutive All-Star Game. His adjusted ERA+ of 143 was the best in baseball that year.

Gary Carter's

11

Postseason RBI

The most important trade the Mets ever made was acquiring perennial All-Star catcher Gary Carter from the Montreal Expos for a package of players in December 1984. Adding the veteran Carter to a group that already featured young stars Dwight Gooden and Darryl Strawberry was seen as the move that put the ascending Mets over the top. "Kid," a nickname Carter picked up in Montreal, controlled the game from behind the plate and routinely provided clutch at-bats, as evidenced by his club-leading 11 postseason RBI in 1986.

An All-American quarterback in high school who also excelled in baseball and basketball, Carter received almost 100 scholarship offers. He sat out his entire senior year due to a knee injury, and in fact was warned by doctors that another bad hit playing football could end his athletic career. Thus baseball became Carter's ticket to stardom. The Expos made Carter their third-round draft pick in 1972. Three years later, he finished runner-up to Giants pitcher John Montefusco for NL Rookie of the Year.

Trade talks between Mets GM Frank Cashen and his counterpart in Montreal, team president John McHale, were long and complicated...mostly because McHale *loved* Carter both as a player and as a person and hated giving him up. The only reason the Expos were finally willing to part with Carter was because they could no longer afford him.

Carter's best years were behind him by the time he arrived in New York, though he still had some prime seasons to give the Mets. He certainly made a great first impression, homering off the Cardinals' Neil Allen in the 10th inning to give the Mets a 6–5 victory on Opening Day, 1985. He became the team's cleanup hitter and got the most out of a dynamic but youthful pitching staff. Everything he did, he did with intensity and exuberance. His smile was as infectious as his desire to win.

The '86 Mets ran away with the division with a 108–54 record. The closest team in the rearview mirror, the Philadelphia Phillies, were 21½ games back. Heading into the playoffs, New York was favored to come out of the National League. First, though, they'd have to get past the Houston Astros in the NLCS.

Although Carter tied Astros first baseman Glenn Davis for the MLB lead in game-winning RBI that season with 16, he did not have a great series at the plate, batting just .148 with four hits and two RBI. But he made them count.

Facing Nolan Ryan in the top of the fourth inning in Game 2, Carter opened the scoring with an RBI double to center-right. In Game 5, he singled off bespectacled reliever Charlie Kerfield in the bottom of the 12th inning to drive in the game-winning run, giving the Mets a 3–2 series lead heading back to Houston. Game 6 went 16 innings and lasted four hours and 42 minutes. Carter had a pair of hits in that one, too, which the Mets won 7–6 to advance to the World Series.

The Red Sox jumped out to a 2–0 series lead before the Mets got back into the series, tagging Oil Can Boyd for six earned runs in Game 3. Carter had an RBI double in the first inning and drove in a pair with a single in the top of the seventh. The Mets won 7–1.

Carter's two-run homer over the Green Monster in the top of the fourth inning of Game 4 put the Mets ahead 2–0. He added another four-bagger in the top of the eighth to widen New York's lead to 5–0.

Game 5 was another beauty by Sox lefty Bruce Hurst, who was now 2–0 in the series. Doc Gooden dropped to 0–2.

Now facing elimination, the Mets were down to their last chance in Game 6, when Carter, who had tied the game in the eighth with a sacrifice fly, came to the plate with two outs and nobody on base in the bottom of the 10th. New York was trailing Boston 5–3 at the time.

MOST SILVER SLUGGER AWARDS AMONG CATCHERS:

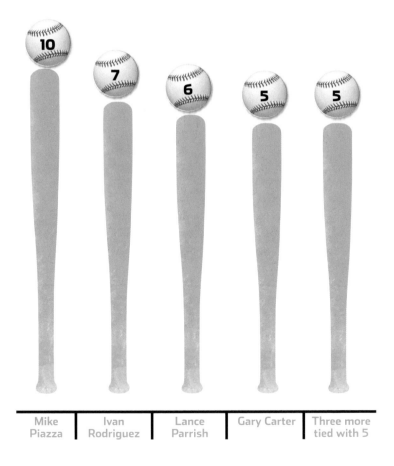

Mike Piazza	Ivan Rodriguez	Lance Parrish	Gary Carter	Three more tied with 5
10	7	6	5	5

Carter was determined not to make the last out of the World Series. Facing reliever Calvin Schiraldi, he fouled off the first pitch, then took the next two for balls. Then came the hit that kicked off the rally that saved the Mets' season: a clean line-drive single to left. Three batters and one slow grounder between Bill Buckner's legs, and the Mets had themselves a 6–5 victory.

In the seventh and decisive game, with the Mets trailing 3–2 in the sixth, Carter drove in the tying run with a grounder to short. It was his ninth RBI of the series and 11th of the postseason.

Game 6 went 16 innings and lasted four hours and 42 minutes.

New York went on to win 8–5 and capture its second World Series title. Nothing came easy for the Mets in the fall of '86, but Kid made it a little easier.

Knee injuries ground Carter down, in part because he always wanted to stay in the lineup. The 11-time All-Star retired in 1992 after 19 years in the league, including five with the Mets. He had a lifetime .262 average with 324 home runs and 1,225 RBI. His 11,785 putouts are the most all-time among catchers.

Inducted into the Baseball Hall of Fame in 2003, Carter stayed in the game as a broadcaster with the Florida Marlins and Expos. He then coached and managed in the minors, independent ball, and college, but his dream of returning to the majors went unfulfilled. He passed away on February 16, 2012, after a bout with brain cancer. He was 57.

"When you think of the great baseball field generals, you think Gary Carter," Hall of Fame president Jeff Idelson said. "He ran the game from behind the plate with strong leadership and passion. The Kid's contribution to our national pastime is big, but his heart was even bigger."

Matt Harvey's

11

Strikeout Debut

The New York Mets had the seventh overall pick in the 2010 draft, which they used to select a tall, strapping pitcher named Matt Harvey. The 6'4" native of New London, Connecticut, had a big personality and an even bigger fastball. It was part of an arsenal of pitches he brought to bear in mowing down 11 batters in his major league debut.

Originally drafted in 2007 by the Angels, he opted against signing with that club and instead decided to go to college. After three years at the University of North Carolina, where he posted a 22–7 record, the right-hander got as high as AA Binghamton in 2011. He also pitched in the MLB Futures Game, an exhibition played during the All-Star break filled with the league's best prospects. In that game, he recorded a save as the U.S. beat the World team.

On July 26, 2012, Harvey made his major league debut against the Arizona Diamondbacks at Chase Field in Phoenix. Over five-plus

Matt Harvey takes the field to start his complete-game, six-strikeout shutout of the Rockies at Citi Field on August 7, 2013. *(Jim McIsaac)*

A 2013 study published in the American Journal of Sports Medicine showed that of 179 major league pitchers who elected to undergo Tommy John surgery, about 97% were eventually able to continue pitching professionally at some level while 83% returned to the majors.

innings, he yielded just three hits and struck out 11 batters—the first Mets rookie to accomplish that feat. He also showed that he could handle a bat, hitting a single and a double. With that, he became the first pitcher in 112 years to get two hits *and* strike out 10 or more batters in his major league debut.

The news traveled fast that Mets fans had a new ace to root for, a homegrown ace. In Harvey's second start, against the Giants, he pitched six innings, struck out seven, and gave up two runs in a 4–1 loss. But with 18 strikeouts in his first two starts, he set another Mets rookie record.

Some Mets fans actually traveled to Great American Ballpark in Cincinnati just to see their new flame-throwing phenom in action. Harvey didn't disappoint, getting his second career win after gutting out an inning in the rain. Harvey was throwing well and he was getting extra-base hits and RBI, contributing more than the Mets could have imagined early on.

He won three games that first season and then the Mets shut him down before the season ended. But they knew they had something to look forward to in 2013.

With much fanfare, Harvey strutted into the next season striking out 19 in his first 14 innings, many times with a 98 MPH heater. He was quickly the talk of the town and the league, winning Pitcher of the Month honors in April. The May 20, 2013, cover of *Sports Illustrated* dubbed him "The Dark Knight of Gotham." Believers in the magazine's so-called "cover jinx" no doubt cringed. A month later, Harvey certainly didn't look jinxed when he took a no-hitter into the seventh inning against the Braves but lost it to an infield hit. He whiffed 13 in that game, a 4–3 Mets win.

Citi Field and the Mets hosted the 2013 All-Star Game. Starting for the National League in his first Midsummer Classic, Harvey thrilled the home crowd by tossing two scoreless innings, giving up just one hit and striking out three: Detroit's Miguel Cabrera, Toronto's Jose Bautista, and Baltimore's Adam Jones.

Harvey discussed his rapid rise to baseball stardom, his love affair with New York City, and other sundry topics over breakfast at a pricey French bistro for a *Men's Journal* exposé. With confidence bordering on cockiness, the 24-year-old bachelor declared his admiration for Derek Jeter of the crosstown rival Yankees, stating, "Look at the women he's dated. Obviously, he goes out—he's meeting these girls somewhere—but you never hear about it. That's where I want to be." Here was the all-too-human side of the fiercely competitive pitcher Mets fans had quickly grown to love.

OF MATT HARVEY'S 106 PITCHES AGAINST THE DIAMONDBACKS, 65 WERE FOR STRIKES

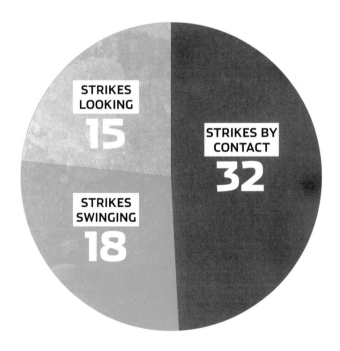

STRIKES LOOKING
15

STRIKES BY CONTACT
32

STRIKES SWINGING
18

The world was Harvey's oyster. And then, three words that strike fear into the hearts of managers: Tommy John surgery. The Mets announced that their ace would undergo the season-ending procedure to repair a partially torn ulnar collateral ligament in his right elbow and miss all of 2014. Harvey's Twitter account nearly exploded after the crushing news went public.

In 26 starts that season, Harvey went 9–5 with a 2.27 ERA, a stellar .931 WHIP, and 191 strikeouts in 178.1 innings—the kind of numbers that earn one consideration for a National League Cy Young (the award eventually went to the Dodgers' Clayton Kershaw).

Harvey whiffed 13 in a 4–3 Mets win.

Harvey had resisted going under the knife for as long as possible and dropped hints about wanting—even expecting—to come back early enough to pitch before the end of the 2014 season, months ahead of schedule. He didn't, and the Mets finished four games under .500. But his eagerness to get back on the mound and pick up right where he left off gave Mets fans one more reason to be excited about the future.

The Year Felix Millan Struck Out Only

14

Times

Felix Millan, the pride of Yabucoa, Puerto Rico, came up at a time when Major League Baseball didn't have an abundance of Latin players. "The Cat" also stood out because, at 5'11", he had a small strike zone, made even smaller by a crouching batting stance. He was a patient hitter, too, adding to his reputation as a tough out. In 1974, Millan was so hard to beat that opposing pitchers struck him out only 14 times in 518 at-bats.

Millan broke into the big leagues in 1966 with the Atlanta Braves. Three years later, he faced his future team, the New York Mets, in the 1969 NLCS, hitting a cool .333 in a losing cause. That year, he won his first Gold Glove at second base and appeared in his first of three consecutive All-Star Games. In July 1970, he set a Braves' club record with six hits in a single game.

On November 2, 1972, Millan and pitcher George Stone were traded to the Mets for fan-favorite Gary Gentry, a hot-tempered, hard-throwing righty, and the late, great reliever Danny Frisella, whose career was cut short in a tragic dune buggy accident in 1977.

Millan was an instant hit with fans (and manager Yogi Berra) because he almost always made contact, ran hard, fielded the ball cleanly, and drove pitchers nuts fouling off copious amounts of pitches. He had a distinctive way of choking up on the bat, so much so that his hands almost divided his already short bat in half. The technique enabled him to spray singles all over the field. In fact, 1,328 of his 1,617 career hits were singles.

He and Stone were two important pieces of the 1973 Mets squad that made it to the World Series, where they blew a 3–2 lead to the powerful Oakland A's and lost in seven games. Millan batted .188 in the series and committed an uncharacteristic error in Game 1 that led to two unearned runs in a 2–1 loss.

By now, it was no secret that the popular infielder was one of the hardest players in baseball to strike out. Although the 1974 Mets stumbled to a 71–91 finish, Millan's plate appearances—specifically, his remarkable ability to avoid the K—offered a ray of sunshine in an otherwise dreary season. He struck out only twice in May, once in June, and not at all from August 21 to September 29, a span of 38 games.

Millan's 14 whiffs is still a Mets record-low for a single season but, amazingly, isn't a major league record. Joe Sewell holds the record for fewest strikeouts over a full season, with three, set in 1930 with the Indians. He repeated the feat in 1932 while playing for the Yankees, albeit in just 353 at-bats (as opposed to 503 in his record-setting year), as well as three other full seasons (1925, 1929, 1933) with just four strikeouts.

THE SACRIFICIAL CAT

In 1974, Felix Millan led the National League with 24 sacrifice bunts.

In 2,677 at-bats, Millan only struck out 92 times, while collecting 743 hits as a .278 batter for the Mets. In 1975, he set the club record (since broken) for hits in a season with 191, while playing in all 162 games—also a Mets record and tops in the National League that year.

On July 21 of that season, Felix hit four singles against the Astros, but he never reached second base. That's because the man batting directly behind him, the veteran Joe Torre, hit into a major league–record four double plays. The nine-time All-Star had lost a step or three in this, his 16th major league season and first with the Mets. Afterwards, Joe famously thanked Felix for making the record possible.

Millan suffered a career-ending shoulder injury in a fight with Pittsburgh's Ed Ott on August 12, 1977.

FELIX MILLAN AT-BATS PER STRIKEOUT

1973 — 29.0

1974 — 37.0

1975 — 24.1

1976 — 27.9

1977 — 34.8

Ventura's
15th
Inning "Grand Slam Single"

The Mets finally had a chance, a *real* chance, to knock their hated rivals from Atlanta off their perch and out of the postseason thanks to a 15-inning, nearly six-hour victory in Game 5 of the 1999 NLCS. That victory was sealed in most dramatic fashion by Robin Ventura's "grand slam single."

In the winter of 1998, the Mets were on the cusp of having a playoff-caliber team but were still in the market for a few more pieces. They found one in Ventura, one of the best-fielding, clutch-hitting third basemen available.

With the Mets trailing 3–1 in the series, Game 5 of the 1999 NLCS certainly looked like a mismatch on paper: New York's Masato Yoshii versus future–Hall of Famer Greg Maddux.

Maddux lasted seven innings, Yoshii just three. That forced Mets manager Bobby Valentine to dig deep into his bullpen. He sent out a parade of relievers—seven in all. Octavio Dotel worked the

Robin Ventura watches his walk-off "grand slam single" clear the fence to beat the Atlanta Braves 4–3 on October 17, 1999, during the National League Championship Series at Shea Stadium. *(Matt Campbell/AFP)*

last three. The score was tied 2–2 at the end of four and the teams remained deadlocked for the next 10 innings. Then Atlanta scored one in the top of the 15th thanks to a Keith Lockhart triple. The Mets needed a miracle and when it came to the Braves, miracles were usually in short supply.

Atlanta's loudmouth reliever, John Rocker, left the game and was replaced by rookie Kevin McGlinchy. Braves skipper Bobby Cox was running out of arms, creating a golden opportunity for the Mets.

Shawon Dunston led off with a single. With Matt Franco, the Mets' best pinch-hitter, at the plate for Dotel, Dunston stole second (even at 36, Dunston could still motor). Franco walked, then Edgardo Alfonzo laid down a sacrifice bunt to advance the runners. McGlinchy loaded the bases by intentionally walking John Olerud, who homered earlier in the game, then walked Todd Pratt, scoring the tying run.

Up walked Ventura, already known for his clutch hitting and propensity for hitting grand slams. Even he couldn't have envisioned what would happen next. Ventura hit a 2-1 ball as well as anyone could. Mets play-by-play man Gary Cohen screamed, "ROBIN VENTURA!" as the ball soared over the fence near the Wiz sign.

A dejected McGlinchy walked off the mound as Ventura trotted the bases. Mets players waiting at home plate to congratulate the hero of the hour couldn't wait any longer and decided to mob Ventura before he could reach second base.

The Mets' official scorer, Howie Karpin, wasn't on duty that night but he was there and remembered confusion in the press box surrounding Ventura's 15th inning game-winner.

"Ventura got a single because Todd Pratt intercepted him after he touched first," Karpin said. "He never touched the other bases. Since the winning run scored from third, Ventura only needed to touch first base to end the game. Thus the term, 'grand slam single.' I actually had to explain to the media members that the final score was 4–3, not 7–3."

The euphoria of that victory was short-lived. The Mets went on to a Game 6, but lost the series in one of the worst ways imaginable: with lefty Kenny Rogers loading the bases and then walking in the winning run in the 11th inning.

ALL-TIME GRAND SLAM LEADERS

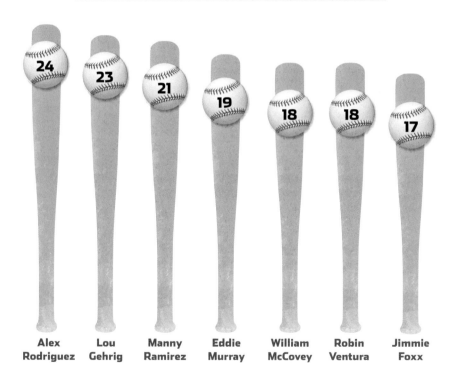

Alex Rodriguez	Lou Gehrig	Manny Ramirez	Eddie Murray	William McCovey	Robin Ventura	Jimmie Foxx
24	23	21	19	18	18	17

Mets Sign

17

Year-Old Dominican Phenom Juan Lagares

When it comes to scouting the baseball stars of tomorrow, discovering that diamond in the rough has long been a source of pride for major league scouts and general managers. The Mets followed the development of Juan Lagares with great interest before signing him as an undrafted 17-year-old out of his native Dominican Republic in 2006. Since then, this diamond in the rough has become the crown jewel of the Mets outfield.

Lagares was signed as a shortstop but converted to an outfielder in 2009. The Mets have long been high on his defense, and in 2014 Lagares showed why by winning the National League Gold Glove. The second-year man became the first Mets outfielder to earn a Gold Glove since Carlos Beltran in 2008 and only the third in franchise history. Tommie Agee won the award in 1970.

Veteran Curtis Granderson, who had just completed his first season playing alongside Lagares, raved to the *Daily News* about his teammate's defensive instincts.

"I was talking to Matt Harvey and Daniel Murphy this off-season," Granderson said. "I don't know how that conversation came up, but someone said something about Gold Gloves. I was like, 'You know what? Juan is by far the best outfielder I've seen, that I've played with and got a chance to watch.' There's some amazing things he does. He's not necessarily the fastest guy out there, but his jumps are amazing. His reads are amazing. He's got the range. He closes the gap."

The Gold Glove has been dismissed by some fans as an overrated award and one that—rightly or wrongly—relies too heavily on statistics to identify the best defensive players at each position.

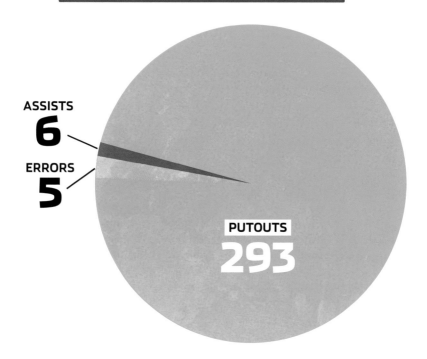

JUAN LAGARES HAD
304 DEFENSIVE CHANCES IN 2014

ASSISTS
6

ERRORS
5

PUTOUTS
293

Sometimes, the magic a player works with his glove can't be quantified numerically. It has to be *seen* to be appreciated. In his brief career, Lagares has thrilled Mets fans by making the seemingly impossible catches look possible.

But, judged on numbers alone, Lagares' defensive statistics made him the obvious choice for the award in 2014. Lagares recorded 293 putouts and finished second among major league outfielders with 28 defensive runs saved, behind the Braves' Jason Heyward.

He finished first among NL outfielders in range factor (2.85) and had a defensive WAR of 3.37. That 3.37 was second in all of baseball, behind only Atlanta's Andrelton Simmons.

> *... finished first among NL outfielders in range factor with **2.85.***

In 2013, his rookie season, Lagares led the NL in assists among outfielders with 14. His assists dropped to six in 2014, in part because fewer batters are testing him.

As many runs as he's saved with his glove, Lagares is starting to produce more runs with his bat and his legs. He batted .281 in 2014, up from .242 the prior season, with 117 hits and a .703 OPS in 116 games (he missed significant time battling hamstring, abdominal muscle, and elbow injuries).

Lagares' Gold Glove was well-deserved. And it will likely not be his last.

 **DID YOU KNOW?** Juan Lagares' 14 outfield assists in 2013 was impressive, but not even close to the major league record. That distinction belongs to Chuck Klein, who had 44 assists in 1930 with the Philadelphia Phillies. That worked out to an outfield assist every 3.9 games—an amazing ratio. Klein had a great throwing arm but was aided by playing right field at Philadelphia's Baker Bowl, which was only 281 feet to right field and 300 to right center.

Marvelous Marv's

17

Errors at First

He was perhaps the most lovable loser on a team of losers. Marv Throneberry was a symbol of the hapless 1962 Mets, a hodgepodge of past-their-prime veterans, career underachievers, and castoffs from the other major league teams. Despite a career-high 17 errors at first base, he managed to develop a cult following.

Nicknamed "Marvelous Marv," Throneberry joined the inaugural Mets after brief stints with the Yankees, Kansas City A's, and Baltimore Orioles. The team won 40 times that year and lost 120. Oddly enough, that season was Throneberry's best: he hit 16 home runs, had 49 RBI, and batted .238.

Many tall tales were told about Marv—some true, some not—but the most famous one involves his shortcomings as a base runner. The oft-told story begins with him hitting what appeared to be a two-out, bases-loaded triple against the Chicago Cubs that would've won the game for New York. But while rounding the bases, he missed touching first. When the Cubs' pitcher tossed the ball to the first baseman, the umpire called Throneberry out. The inning ended and the runs didn't count. An incredulous Casey Stengel came out of the dugout to argue the call with the first-base umpire. Supposedly, as the two exchanged words, another umpire walked over and told the Mets manager, "Casey, I hate to tell you this, but he also missed second."

Marvelous Marv didn't do the Mets many favors with his glove, either. Of the 34 errors he committed in his major league career, exactly half came in 1962. Apart from that one brutal year with the Mets, Throneberry was no worse than average with a career fielding percentage of .987 as a first baseman. In fact, the Yankees occasionally used him a defensive replacement.

It's been said that whenever Stengel complained aloud, "Can't anybody here play this game?" (a quote that would become the title of Jimmy Breslin's famous book about the '62 Mets), he was really directing the question at Throneberry.

In 1963, Throneberry got off to a slow start and was demoted to Triple-A Buffalo to make room for another Met legend, Ed Kranepool. He was eventually released from the team and retired at age 29. In seven major league seasons, he was a .237 hitter with 53 home runs and 170 RBI in 480 games.

Throneberry, who died in 1994 at age 60 following a bout with cancer, had a good sense of humor about his lackluster career. After he retired, he poked fun at himself in a series of Miller Lite beer commercials. In one, he deadpanned, "I'm kinda worried because if I do for light beer what I did for baseball, I'm afraid their sales might go down."

 The all-time record for most errors in a season by a first baseman belongs to the legendary Cap Anson, who had 58 playing for the 1884 White Stockings. Anson also holds the career mark for errors by a first baseman with 568.

Amazin' for

18

Seasons: Ed Kranepool

One of the earliest signings of the expansion Mets was a 17-year-old kid out of James Monroe High School in the Bronx. No one could have predicted that Ed Kranepool would play more games as a Met than anyone else in the history of the franchise.

Oh, the Mets have had quite a few better hitters—Mike Piazza, Darryl Strawberry, and Keith Hernandez, to name just a few—but none of them had the opportunity to compile 1,418 hits over 18 seasons.

Ed's father died in 1944 while serving in World War II. His mother was six months pregnant with Ed at the time. Forced to raise two young kids on a small military widow's pension, she had to work odd jobs to keep the family afloat.

A two-sport star in high school, Ed turned down basketball scholarships from St John's University and North Carolina. The lefty-hitting first baseman began his professional baseball career in the minors where he excelled through three levels. Hitting a hair over .300, he earned a call-up to the Mets on September 22, 1962. The youngest player by far on a team populated with aging veterans, he played only three games and had six plate appearances. It was just a taste of the challenges yet to come.

The Mets liked Ed's versatility. In 1963, he split time with one of the great characters of the game, "Marvelous" Marv Throneberry, at first base, and the former Brooklyn Dodger great, Duke Snider, in right field. Throneberry lasted only 23 games before being demoted, giving more playing time to Kranepool at first base, a position he was better suited for behind Tim Harkness.

The following year, despite spending part of the season with the Triple-A Buffalo Bisons, Kranepool finally made a case for himself as a full-time major leaguer. He hit his way back to the bigs and played in 119 games, including a 23-inning marathon versus San Francisco on May 31, 1964. Entrenched at first base, with an occasional turn in the outfield, he hit double-digit home runs in each of the next four seasons.

In 1965, Ed gave up his No. 21 to legendary pitcher Warren Spahn. He wore No. 7 at his first and only All-Star Game, and for the rest of his career. On a roster featuring stars and future Hall of Famers like Willie Mays, Roberto Clemente, Joe Torre, Hank Aaron, Sandy Koufax, and Willie Stargell, Kranepool never even got into the game. But he was on the winning side as the NL defeated the AL 6–5.

In the late 1960s, the Mets' rising star moved to South Farmingdale, New York, where he became a part of the community. At a time when the median household income in the U.S. was about $7,700, Kranepool was living large on a whopping $25,000 salary. Eventually, he scored endorsement deals for Gillette foamy shaving cream and Sports Phone, a 24-hour service that gave 'round-the-clock sports scores. Through it all, he still had an air of the "everyman"—an ordinary guy who just happened to play baseball for

DID YOU KNOW?

Ed Kranepool and Ron Swoboda co-owned a restaurant and lounge on Broadway in North Amityville called The Dugout.

ED KRANEPOOL:
GAMES STARTED VS. GAMES AS A SUBSTITUTE

= GAMES STARTED   = GAMES AS A SUBSTITUTE

1,379
GAMES
STARTED

474 GAMES
AS A
SUBSTITUTE

the Mets. A generation of kids on Long Island grew up watching him play.

In 1969, at the tender age of 24, Kranepool opened the season as the club's veteran first baseman. His two-homer performance against the Dodgers on June 3 extended a winning streak that would reach 11 games, nudged the Mets over .500, and moved them into second place behind the Cubs. Known for his clutch performances at the plate, especially as a pinch hitter, Kranepool had some key hits in a pivotal series against first-place Chicago, including an RBI single on July 8 that won the game in front of 55,000 home fans. The Mets took two of three to win the series—doubly gratifying since some Cubs players had disrespected the Mets in the newspapers by calling them an "inferior" team.

Kranepool played in all three games of the NLCS as the Mets beat the Atlanta Braves, but started only one game of the 1969 World Series. The Mets had another first baseman, Donn Clendenon, who would hit .357 with three homers and be named World Series MVP. Kranepool did hit a nice home run in the eighth inning of Game 3, a game the Mets won 5–0 en route to their first championship.

Despite his status as a sentimental favorite of both the team owner and the fans, this original Met found himself crowded out of the lineup by three other first basemen—Clendenon, Art Shamsky, and rookie Mike Jorgensen—and he was demoted to Tidewater in June 1970. He'd actually been placed on waivers first, but went unclaimed by every other team in the National League thanks to his high salary and low batting average.

IN A PINCH, GET KRANEPOOL

David Wright has rewritten the Mets' record book but there is one mark he's unlikely to eclipse: Ed Kranepool's record for most pinch hits in team history. Kranepool amassed 90 of them, including 17 in 1974, when he hit .486 as a pinch hitter, the highest batting average ever for someone with 30 or more pinch-hit at-bats in a season. Six of those 90 pinch hits were home runs. Fittingly, his 1,418th and final career hit, on September 30, 1979, came while pinch hitting for middle reliever John Pacella.

Hurt and angry, Ed was determined to play his way back onto the Mets...which he did the following spring, and never spent another day in the minors.

The Mets were back in the postseason in 1973. Starting in place of the injured Rusty Staub, Kranepool hit a two-run single in New York's 7–2 win over Cincinnati in Game 5 of the NLCS. Appearing in only four games of the World Series, he went hitless in three at-bats as Oakland took the series in seven games.

At a time when the median household income in the U.S. was about $7,700, Kranepool was living large on a whopping $25,000 salary.

In 1977, contract squabbles with general manager Joe McDonald left Krane feeling a bit underappreciated—McDonald didn't give Kranepool the time it took to get home before rescinding an offer—but team chairman M. Donald Grant stepped in and signed Kranepool to a new three-year deal, and even threw in a $10,000 bonus.

Two years later, at age 34, Ed decided to call it quits. Many of the club records he once held have since fallen, but his 18 seasons is a mark that should stand for many years to come.

Doc Wins

24

When Dwight Gooden was coming through the Mets minor league system there was considerable buzz. This wasn't New York "hype," this was excitement for the kind of pitcher that comes along once every decade. With a curveball that would fall off the table and heat in the high 90s, the pride of Hillsborough High in Tampa, Florida, was the youngest Met to win 24 games.

It was pretty clear that the 1983 Lynchburg Mets had the best pitcher in the minors. Gooden was the Class A player of the year, and his manager, future Mets third-base coach Sam Perlozzo, was the manager of the year. The big club needed some help. They owned the National League's worst record at 68–94.

Gooden made the jump, along with AAA manager Davey Johnson, and the tall, lanky right-hander had an instant impact. On April 7, 1984, at the tender age of 19, he toed the rubber at the Houston Astrodome, pitched five, struck out five, and got his first of many wins that July. He became the youngest player to appear in an All-Star game. He struck out 16 batters twice that year and led baseball with 276. He won 17 games and came in second in the Cy

Doc Gooden pitches during his amazing 1985 season. *(Ronald C. Modra)*

Young Award voting. The Mets phenom did win the Rookie of the Year Award.

"As a young pitcher you focus on making the team. I was very excited and my dad was very excited. You don't think about winning awards. You don't think about winning the Rookie of the Year Award, but when you do it's pretty special," said Gooden.

The Mets had expectations placed on them in the spring of 1985 because of the acquisition of Gary Carter. Some thought Gooden and Carter could be the best battery in baseball. Keith Hernandez said he felt like the Cubs were still the favorite but the Mets were in the conversation.

"Gary Carter was amazing; he would just setup and you would throw to him," Gooden said.

Number 16 was loaded with confidence heading into the '85 campaign. Along with Ron Darling, Sid Fernandez, and Rick Aguilera, the Mets starters were young but talented.

DOC GOODEN'S 1985 HOME/ROAD WINS

= HOME   = ROAD

13 WINS AT HOME

11 WINS ON THE ROAD

From May 30 through August 25, 1985, "Dr. K" reeled off 14 wins without a loss. Ten of them were complete games and four of them were shutouts. By August 25, he was an unbelievable 20–3. He finished the season winning his last four starts with a 24–4 record, the youngest Met to win 20 or more games.

The Mets finished in second place with 98 wins, but they were three games behind the division-winning St. Louis Cardinals. Gooden won the Cy Young over the Cardinals John Tudor.

He struck out 16 batters twice that year and led baseball with 276.

He was on his second All-Star team and he won the Triple Crown of pitching. For the second consecutive season, he led the majors in strikeouts. He was arguably the best pitcher in the game.

Gooden was the Mets ace for many years to come. He still holds Met records for most right-handed rookie wins with 17 and shutouts in a season with eight. He had a great NLCS in '86, but he was 0–2 in the Fall Classic. As his numbers went up and down it had to do with his off-field issues with addiction.

Gooden gave up the "home run heard around New York" to light-hitting catcher Mike Scioscia in Game 4 of the 1988 NLCS. The Dodgers tied up that game and won in 12 innings. The Mets could have been up 3–1 in the series but instead it evened up. The Mets eventually lost that series 4–3. The once-dominant ace of the Mets never pitched in a Flushing postseason after that series.

After that Gooden had some very nice seasons, just not dominant. His fastball was starting to fade. He threw a no-hitter for the New York Yankees in 1996. He also managed to get two more World Series rings with the Yankees but he wasn't a major contributor. Today, Doc is staying clean and sober and making personal appearances for various entities. He also shares his message of hope to anybody who'll listen.

No. 24 Was a

24

Time All-Star

Willie Mays returned to the city where his Hall of Fame career began two decades earlier when the Mets acquired him from the San Francisco Giants in May 1972 for pitching-prospect (and Flushing-native) Charlie Williams and $50,000.

The last-place Giants didn't send Mays back to New York to finish his career solely out of the kindness of their hearts, although that was part of their motivation. Mostly, they were tired of paying Willie top dollar for rapidly diminishing returns—Mays was batting just .182 with no home runs—and didn't want to guarantee him a lucrative coaching job when his playing days were over. But Mets owner and president Joan Payson, a former minority owner of the Giants who absolutely adored Mays, was willing to give him the long-term security he craved. And Payson hoped that having such a durable box-office attraction would lure back some of the 500,000-plus customers the Mets had lost over the previous two seasons.

The team barely made any effort to spin the trade as anything but a PR stunt.

"I hope this move will be successful at the gate," Mets chairman M. Donald Grant confessed. "It'd be hard to deny that getting Willie Mays might prove to be rewarding. But that simply wasn't our purpose. We feel that there's a lot of sentiment and pride in this [trade]."

Ironically, Willie's first game with the Mets—on Mother's Day—was against his former team. Manager Yogi Berra, with whom Mays would eventually spar over playing time, slotted his newest acquisition in at first base. Batting leadoff, and wearing his familiar No. 24, Mays drew a walk in his first trip to the plate. He scored a run a few moments later when Rusty Staub hit a grand slam off Sam McDowell to put New York ahead 4–0. Within the span of just five pitches at the top of the fifth inning, San Francisco stormed back to tie the game. In the bottom of the fifth, Mays had a full count when he drilled a pitch from Don Carrithers over the left-field fence. That dramatic home run, his first of the season and first as a Met, turned out to be the game-winner.

Moments like that, increasingly few and far between for the fading legend, reminded older Mets fans of the good old days when Mays dominated the Polo Grounds with his bat and his glove. In his prime, Mays made a case as the best all-around ballplayer on the planet. The two-time National League MVP had a career batting average of .302, drove in over 100 runs for eight consecutive seasons, and is currently fourth on the all-time list with 660 home runs. A 12-

BANNED BY BOWIE

In 1979, in an effort to distance Major League Baseball from anything related to gambling, Bowie Kuhn banned Willie Mays from working in baseball after Mays signed a 10-year deal to do public relations for the Bally's casino in Atlantic City. At the time, Mays was earning $50,000 a year as a coach for the Mets (one always knew when Willie was at work because his pink Chrysler Imperial with "SAY HEY" vanity plates would be parked outside the stadium). The ban on Mays—and a similar one imposed on Mickey Mantle—was lifted six years later by new commissioner Peter Ueberroth.

time Gold Glove winner, he compiled 7,095 putouts—the all-time record for an outfielder. Joe DiMaggio once said Mays had the greatest throwing arm in baseball.

But that Willie Mays wasn't the one representing the Mets at the 1973 All-Star Game in Kansas City. At 42, the Say Hey Kid was a broken-down player who'd close out his 22nd and final major league season batting .211 with six home runs. There really was no way to justify his inclusion at the Midsummer Classic—he'd rightly been left off the original 28-man roster—but sentiment trumped merit when Commissioner Bowie Kuhn added Mays at the last minute. It was Mays' 24th All-Star appearance in 20 seasons, a record he shares with Hank Aaron and Stan Musial (in the four years from 1959 to 1962, two All-Star games were played each season). He was in the starting line-up for 18 of those games, always playing center field.

Two months later, just prior to the next-to-last home game of the season, the Mets and their fans said goodbye to an unforgettable era of baseball. DiMaggio, Duke Snider, and Stan Musial were just a few of the big names from the past who showed up for Willie Mays Night, a bittersweet affair in which the Mets and their sponsors showered Willie and his wife, Mae, with gifts. There was the white mink coat (for her), a pile of golf bags and equipment (for him), a trip around the world, and three cars, including one from Giants owner Horace Stoneham.

Homemade banners dotted the stands. One read "Willie, We'll Never Forget You." "A Giant Among Mets" read another. "Say Hey Belongs to Shea" was the most lyrical.

"This is a sad day for me," an emotional Mays told the crowd. "I may not look it, but it is a new experience for me to have you cheer for me and not be able to do anything about it."

Mets Lose

25

Inning Game

On September 11, 1974, the Mets and Cardinals played the second-longest major league game on record: a 25-inning marathon at Shea Stadium that began shortly after 8:00 PM and didn't end until 3:13 AM the following morning.

The game, which the Cardinals won 4–3, involved 50 players and required 15 dozen baseballs, five sweepings of the infield, and an incalculable number of bathroom breaks. Even at seven hours and five minutes, the game wasn't the longest in elapsed time. It fell 19 minutes short of the record set by the Mets and San Francisco Giants on May 31, 1964.

Joe Torre put the Cardinals on the board early with an RBI single off Jerry Koosman in the first inning. New York answered quickly when John Milner's double to right in the bottom of the inning scored Cleon Jones. In the bottom of the fifth, Jones hit a two-run homer off Bob Forsch, putting the Mets ahead 3–1.

The game might have ended at a respectable hour if not for the Cards' Ken Reitz, who hit a two-run homer over the left-field fence with two outs in the ninth, tying it up at three runs apiece. New York failed to score another run in the bottom of the ninth.

As the game pushed deep into extra innings, the Mets would remain scoreless for 20 innings—long enough to play over two "normal" games. Through it all, the Diamond Club stayed open for hungry fans, long after the hot dog vendors had called it a night.

"It was a good crowd," Mets executive Jim Thomson said. "One guy was even dancing in the aisles every inning in right field. It amazes me that people stay that late. At 3:00 in the morning, you had a chant of 'Let's go, Mets!' You didn't have it by many people, but you had it."

LONGEST GAMES IN MAJOR LEAGUE HISTORY

Brooklyn Robins 1 at Boston Braves 1 (5/1/1920)	**26** INNINGS
St. Louis Cardinals 4 at New York Mets 3 (9/11/1974)	**25** INNINGS
Chicago White Sox 7 vs. Milwaukee Brewers 6 (5/8/1984)	**25** INNINGS
Philadelphia A's 4 at Boston Americans 1 (9/1/1906)	**24** INNINGS
Detroit Tigers 1 at Philadelphia A's 1 (7/21/1945)	**24** INNINGS
Houston Astros 1 vs. New York Mets 0 (4/15/1968)	**24** INNINGS

New York's Dave Schneck tied a single-game major league record with 11 at-bats. He doubled twice and struck out three times. As a team, the Mets also set club records for most at-bats (89) and most men left on base (25).

About 1,000 of the original announced crowd of 13,460 were dedicated (or crazy) enough to stay for the entire game. The end mercifully came when Bake McBride score the winning run for St. Louis on a wild pickoff throw by Mets reliever Hank Webb and a fumbled throw home by catcher Ron Hodges.

"Why does it always happen to me?" home plate umpire Ed Sudol groaned to a reporter after having called every pitch thrown to the record total of 202 batters. Sudol also worked the 23-inning game between the Mets and Giants in 1964 and a Mets-Astros game in 1968 that went 24 innings.

Sudol was probably feeling a little cranky when he ejected Mets manager Yogi Berra from the game around 1:30 AM, during a heated argument over a called strike to Wayne Garrett.

> **About 1,000 of the original announced crowd of 13,460 were dedicated (or crazy) enough to stay for the entire game.**

Yogi, who always had a way with words, was asked how it felt to be part of such an historic sporting event.

"How does it feel? It feels bad," he said. "If you play 25 innings and win, you feel a lot better than when you play 25 and lose."

Anthony Young's

27

Game Losing Streak

Ballplayers are like the rest of us: they all want to be remembered. Some are lucky enough to be remembered for their accomplishments. Others, for their failures. It's in the latter regard that pitcher Anthony Young staked his claim to fame, setting a major league record by dropping 27 consecutive decisions.

The hard-throwing righty seemed to be one of those feel-good stories when he debuted for the Mets at Shea on August 5, 1991, a little over four years after he was drafted in the 38th round out of the University of Houston. At 25, with four seasons of minor league ball to his name, Young looked like he was ready for major league duty. He pitched two innings of relief against the Cubs, giving up one run in a 7–2 loss. The team eventually found room for Young in the starting rotation and he won a few games, but he quickly became a hard-luck pitcher, losing his last four games and going 2–5 on the season, with a respectable 3.10 ERA.

Coming into spring training there was no way the Mets or Young could know what was on the horizon for the Houston native in his sophomore season. After going 2–0 with a complete-game victory under his belt for the month of April, 1992 was looking better. Things turned quickly for Young and by the end of June he was 2–8 with some no-decisions. Then he switched back to the bullpen and he started to get saves as a closer, filling in for the injured John Franco. By the end of July he was 2–9, but he notched seven saves. He was finally reaching his potential.

In August he got three saves, two holds, and no losses. However, he managed to get five more losses in September and finished 2–14. Some teams would cut or trade a player with bad luck or waning talent, but not the Mets. They gave him another chance.

*Over his streak he had converted **12 straight saves** and had a 23²/₃ consecutive scoreless streak, so his teammates were partly to blame.*

By June of 1993, Young was known for losses. At the end of the month he was 0–10. On June 24, that 10ᵗʰ loss put him in a league of his own, breaking the major league record for losing 24 consecutive decisions.

He tacked on three more losses (still a Mets and major league record at 27) but on July 28, after a one-inning relief appearance, he finally got a win. After that game, Young had a wide range of emotions. He must have felt like he had a weight lifted off his back—cue the famous idiom.

"It wasn't a monkey," he said to a *Newsday* reporter. "It was a zoo. I'm glad the zoo is off."

Over 24,000 hometown fans cheered this win. He'd earned that, but after two more starts and another loss he took his 1–16 record to the Windy City and the Cubs after the Mets traded him over the winter. He pitched better for the Cubs but did start out with an 0–2 record. After two seasons with Chicago and one with the Houston

Astros he was done. Injuries and losses did him in. He had a 15–48 career record with a respectable 3.89 ERA. Over his streak he had converted 12 straight saves and had 23⅔ consecutive scoreless innings, so his teammates were partly to blame. During the streak he was 0–14 as a starter and 0–13 as a reliever.

Young's _5–35_ career record with the Mets made him a celebrity.

Now he's a coach and he offers pitching lessons in his home state of Texas. His 5–35 career record with the Mets made him a celebrity. He will tell anybody willing to listen that he owns a record that may never be broken.

Young could have been losing all those games for the now defunct Montreal Expos. They drafted him out of high school in 1984, but he never signed with them.

Dickey's Scoreless Streak Reaches

32.2

Innings

In 2012, the Mets got off to a hot start on the back of R.A. Dickey and carried it all the way to the All-Star break. Midway through the first half, the knuckleball-throwing righty set a new Mets franchise record of 32.2 consecutive scoreless innings, besting Jerry Koosman's 31.2 in 1973.

The streak began on May 22 in Pittsburgh, where Dickey seemed to discover a new mastery over his signature pitch, striking out 11 batters. And it ended a month later, on June 24 against the Yankees at Shea Stadium.

He'd entered the game as the only pitcher in modern major league history (since 1900) to pitch back-to-back complete games allowing one or no hits and striking out at least 10. But in the third inning, he gave up a run on a sacrifice fly by Mark Teixeira, then Nick Swisher followed with a three-run homer—the first earned runs against Dickey since May 22. The Yanks went on to win 6–5.

Dickey's magnificent first half performance earned him his first career All-Star selection. On August 9, he tossed his league-best fourth complete game of the season and allowed just one run while striking out 10 for his sixth double-digit strikeout game of the year. On August 31 at Miami, he earned his 17th win of the season by pitching a five-hit complete game shutout, his third of the year.

On September 27, 2012, the Mets' final home game of the season, Dickey won his 20th game of the season against the Pittsburgh Pirates. He was the Mets' first 20-game winner in 22 years—Frank Viola did it in 1990—and the first knuckleballer to win 20 since Houston's Joe Niekro in 1980.

On the heels of that milestone, plus a 2.73 ERA and league-best 230 strikeouts, Dickey won the NL Cy Young Award, beating out Washington's Gio Gonzalez and Clayton Kershaw of the Dodgers. Along with Gooden and Tom Seaver, he was the third Met but the first knuckleballer in MLB history to win the award. At 37, Dickey had finally reached the top of his profession, all thanks to a high-risk, high-reward pitch.

An effective knuckleball—one with just a little bit of spin—can be unhittable. Dickey has the ability to make the ball dance all around

ORIGINS OF THE KNUCKLEBALL

Lew "Hicks" Moren has been credited as the knuckleball's inventor, dating back to a 1908 article appearing in the *New York Press*. After two games in two seasons with the Pirates from 1903 to 1904, Moren developed the pitch while playing in the minors. When he returned to the major leagues in 1907 with the Phillies, he surprised opponents with his knuckleball. However, some baseball historians believe that Eddie "Knuckles" Cicotte was the true father of the pitch. According to *The New Yorker*, Cicotte discovered early in his career that by pressing the knuckles of his middle and index fingers against the ball's surface, and steadying the ball with his thumb, he could produce a spinless pitch, which would behave erratically and set batters on edge. Cicotte wasn't exclusively a knuckleball pitcher. Even if he didn't invent it, he very likely perfected it.

Although he's the first knuckleballer to win a Cy Young, R.A. Dickey has some catching up to do in the wins department. His 89 career victories is well short of the all-time leader in that category, Hall-of-Famer Phil Niekro.

Wins	Player
318	Phil Niekro
260	Ted Lyons
221	Joe Niekro
216	Charlie Hough
210	Jesse "Pop" Haines
208	Eddie Cicotte
200	Tim Wakefield

the strike zone while changing speeds as well. The speed range may not be as much as from a fastball to a changeup, but it is still significant enough to throw a hitter off balance and ruin his timing. On the other hand, a knuckleball that doesn't break and just hovers there in the strike zone is like a gift-wrapped home run.

"I think guys who played with [Tim] Wakefield would say it was a legitimate pitch," said Ricki Stern, co-director and producer of the 2011 documentary *Knuckleball!* that featured conversations with some of the great knuckleball pitchers of the past and present. "There are guys who hate to bat against it so there is clearly a mixed bag. There is so much emphasis on the radar gun and the pitchers who throw hard get that big money. I think people now, maybe because of R.A., are now really attracted to the pitch."

A Nashville native, Dickey was drafted by the Texas Rangers in 1996 out of the University of Tennessee. Right before his rookie season of 2001, it was discovered that his right arm, his pitching arm, did not have an ulnar collateral ligament, the primary stabilizer of the elbow. When that happened, Dickey's stock as a pitching prospect plummeted. He spent a decade bouncing around—from Texas to

DID YOU KNOW? In the same game that R.A. Dickey's streak of consecutive scoreless innings ended, his stretch of 44$^{2}/_{3}$ innings without allowing an earned run was also broken. He fell 4$^{1}/_{3}$ innings short of matching the franchise record for innings without allowing an earned run, set by Dwight Gooden in 1985.

Seattle to Minnesota—and learned along the way how to throw the knuckleball as a last-ditch effort to keep his career alive. In 2010, he signed with the Mets.

Something about orange and blue agreed with Dickey, and he posted what were then career highs in games started (26), wins (11), complete games (two), innings pitched (174.1), strikeouts (104), ERA (2.84), and even batting average (.252).

He finished the 2011 season with a record of only 8–13, despite an impressive 3.28 ERA that was 12th best in the National League.

It was easy to root for Dickey. Apart from his inspirational journey from relative obscurity to major league star, he was one of the most insightful and eloquent athletes around. He authored a book, *Wherever I Wind Up*, in which he bravely revealed that he was a sexual-abuse victim as a child. He named his bats after swords used in *The Hobbit* and *Beowulf*. And he climbed Mount Kilimanjaro in Tanzania to raise awareness for the Bombay Teen Challenge.

After his Cy Young–winning season, Dickey sought a contract extension from the Mets that would have included a massive raise. Unwilling to meet the pitcher's asking price, the team traded Dickey to the Blue Jays in a seven-player deal.

Workhorse Fisher First Met to Start

36
Games

Baseball in 1965 was, obviously, much different than the game we know today. There were no one-inning specialists like set-up men or closers. In fact, Major League Baseball didn't even track saves as an official statistic until 1969. Managers were only just beginning to see the value of a deep bullpen. Starting pitchers were no longer expected to go the distance, but they still carried heavy workloads. That's how Jack Fisher ended up becoming the first Met to start 36 games in a season. Too bad most of those games ended in defeat.

"Fat Jack," as he was known, weighed 215 pounds but had a stocky frame. As a 21-year-old pitching for the Baltimore Orioles, he surrendered Ted Williams' 521st and final career home run. He was also on the mound when Yankees slugger Roger Maris hit his 60th home run of the 1961 season, tying him with the immortal Babe Ruth.

Acquired by the lowly Mets in 1963, Fisher made an almost immediate impression on the hometown fans by opening their new Shea Stadium on April 17, 1964, against the Pirates. In addition to throwing the first pitch—a strike—Fisher also yielded the first hit—and home run, a towering second-inning blast by Willie Stargell. New York lost that game, 4–3.

The '65 Mets carried only three starting pitchers and it's a toss-up as to who was the ace of the staff: Fisher or Al Jackson, each of whom won only eight games. It certainly wasn't 44-year-old Warren Spahn, the legendary lefty who went 4–12 for the Mets in his final major league season.

> *Fisher pitched a career-high **253 innings** that season, had **10** complete games, and a team-best **ERA** of **3.94.***

Fisher pitched a career-high 253 innings that season, had 10 complete games, and a team-best ERA of 3.94. In addition to his 36 starts he also had seven relief appearances. His 24 losses led the National League and tied him with ex-Met Roger Craig for the most since 1935. The Mets went 50–112 and again finished last in the National League, 47 games behind the pennant-winning Dodgers.

With limited run support, Fisher would lead the league in losses again in 1967 with 18.

The unflappable Casey Stengel was in his fourth and final season as Mets skipper. At 74, Casey still had plenty of moxie but was also easygoing enough to accommodate what was, at the time, an unusual request.

"I asked Casey if it was okay to warm up in the bullpen [instead of on the field] to get away from the hustle and bustle and all the writers," Fisher recalled for the *Daily News*. "I guess I started something."

One of the few pleasant memories Fisher had of his time with the Mets occurred on June 21, 1967, when he pitched the lowest-hit complete game of his career, a two-hit shutout over the Philadelphia Phillies at Connie Mack Stadium.

Having thrown the first pitch in the history of Shea Stadium, Fisher had hoped to throw out the ceremonial first pitch at Citi Field when it opened in 2009, but that honor went to Tom Seaver. Ironically, it was Seaver who matched Fisher's club record for starts in a season in 1970, 1973, and 1975.

Fisher retired in 1969 with a career record of 86–139 (.382). He settled in Easton, Pennsylvania, and opened a sports bar called Fat Jack's, which he later sold.

Todd Hundley's Record-Breaking

41

Home Runs

Growing up in Palatine, Illinois, this second-generation backstop hoped to follow in the footsteps of his father, Randy Hundley, a former major league catcher in the 1960s and '70s. Todd did that and more, eventually passing the legendary Roy Campanella in the record books.

In 1987, the Mets drafted the younger Hundley in the second round, 39th overall, with a pick they acquired from the Baltimore Orioles as compensation for signing third baseman Ray Knight, the 1986 World Series MVP with whom the Mets could never come to terms.

After attending a small junior college, Hundley broke into the majors at the age of 20 in 1990 wearing the same No. 9 as his father. He only played in 36 games because the Mets had a logjam at the position. In 1992, he started to show the kind of promise that would eventually make him the Mets full-time catcher for years to come.

Although injuries slowed his development, he was a rarity in that only 82 switch-hitting catchers had ever played in the history of the game. Only 29 had at least 1,000 career plate appearances, a mark Hundley would eventually pass. He was a tireless worker but he wasn't getting the results he wanted at the plate. Still, he managed to be a solid game manager for pitchers like Dwight Gooden and Bret Saberhagen.

Heading into 1996, few in the baseball world could have imagined what was going to happen next. Hundley had his first All-Star selection but nobody was talking about him breaking a 43-year-old record. Then, on September 9, 1996, the Mets' homegrown star became must-see TV by tying the all-time single-season mark for home runs by a catcher with his 40th homer of the season against the Atlanta Braves (in 1953, the Dodgers' Campanella hit 41 home runs, but 40 in games in which he appeared as a catcher).

Hundley's 419-foot blast also set the Mets' team record, previously set twice (1987 and 1988) by Darryl Strawberry. Hundley was the ninth player that season to hit 40 homers, breaking the Major League Baseball record of eight set in 1961.

Hundley moved past Campanella six days later with a three-run jack, again

TODD HUNDLEY SEASON-BY-SEASON HOME RUNS

Year	Home Runs
1990	0
1991	1
1992	7
1993	11
1994	16
1995	15
1996	41
1997	30
1998	3
1999	24
2000	24
2001	12
2002	16
2003	2

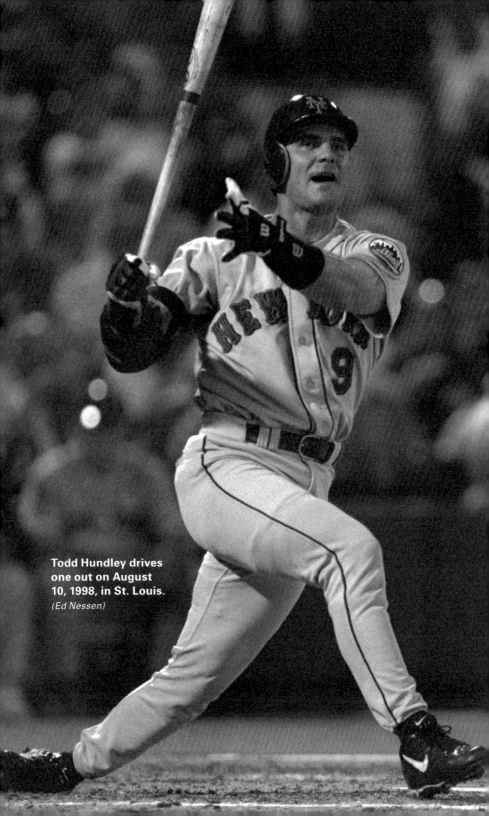

Todd Hundley drives
one out on August
10, 1998, in St. Louis.
(Ed Nessen)

against the Braves. Afterwards, manager Bobby Valentine and teammates drank a toast to Todd out of Styrofoam cups filled with champagne. He finished the season with 41 home runs, 112 RBI, and a mention in MVP balloting.

After suffering an elbow injury during the 1997 season, Hundley underwent Tommy John surgery. When he returned to thunderous applause in the middle of the 1998 season, he was now the second-best catcher on the team behind newly acquired Mike Piazza. After quickly discovering during some minor league games that Hundley wasn't cut out for first base, the Mets moved him to the outfield. He wasn't much better there and he eventually became a pinch-hitter and part-time catcher. With nowhere else to go but up, the Mets traded Hundley to the Dodgers.

> *Huntley finished the season with 41 home runs, 112 RBI, and a mention in MVP balloting.*

In two seasons on the left coast, he did manage consecutive 24-homer seasons before becoming a free agent. A two-year stint with his hometown Cubs followed, but by then his power had greatly diminished. Dealt back to the Dodgers in 2003, he played one more season before calling it quits.

Why the sudden, dramatic decline? Nearly a decade later, the baseball world would have its answer.

In 2011, Major League Baseball commissioned an investigation into the illegal use of steroids and other performance-enhancing substances, also known as the Mitchell Report. Hundley's name appeared in the report. Federal snitch Kirk Radomski testified that he distributed illegal substances to dozens of major leaguers from 1996 to 2005 while working as a clubhouse assistant for the Mets. Page 163 of the Mitchell Report severely tarnished Hundley's record-breaking season in New York, detailing how Radomski had sold an anabolic steroid called DecaDurabolin and testosterone to Hundley on several occasions. At the beginning of that year,

Radomski had told Hundley that if he used steroids, he would hit 40 home runs. Hundley hit 41, having never hit more than 16 in any previous season. After the season, Radomski said, Hundley took him out for a celebratory dinner.

In exchange for his cooperation with the investigation, Radomski got a reduced sentence—from a possible 25-year term to just five years of probation and a fine of $18,575. Hundley's reputation took a beating but he still retains his Mets record.

Dealt back to the Dodgers in 2003, he played **one more season** *before calling it quits.*

Carlos Beltran tied his Mets single-season home run mark in 2006. And Braves catcher Javy Lopez set a new catcher's home run record with 42 in 2003.

Hundley's mention in the Mitchell Report cast a shadow over his career, but he is still revered by many Mets fans. His 40th and 41st home runs in 1996 delivered a much-needed but temporary charge into a fan base searching for a big star to rally behind. They found one, briefly.

Bob Murphy:

42

Years Behind the Mike

Bob Murphy was the radio voice of the Mets for an amazing 42 seasons. He was there at the very beginning, part of a broadcast team that also included Lindsey Nelson and Ralph Kiner, calling the action as he saw it in his distinctive Midwestern baritone until his retirement in 2003.

An Oklahoma native, Murphy worked as a baseball broadcaster for 50 years, starting with the Boston Red Sox in 1954 (where he was partnered with the legendary Curt Gowdy) before moving to the Baltimore Orioles in 1960. It was his memorable call of Roger Maris' 60th home run that was used as an audition tape to land a job calling games for the expansion Mets.

Mets fans got to know the new team and its players by listening to Murphy, who worked both television and radio broadcasts before switching to radio full-time in 1981. He traveled with families in their cars and to the beach. His was "the Voice of Summer"—

comfortable, friendly, and reassuring. Murph was everybody's smart but non-judgmental baseball pal.

His most famous catchphrase, "Stay tuned for the Happy Recap," underscored how he almost always looked for the silver lining in any situation. He rarely had anything negative to say about any team or player. His propensity for staying upbeat came in handy, especially in the early years when the Mets were atrocious.

It wasn't just a job for Murphy. He loved the Mets. He rooted for the Mets. You could hear it in his voice at the end of that 1990 game against the Phillies. New York was leading 10–3 in the ninth when the Phillies scored six runs to make it 10–9. On the final play, a relieved Murphy bellowed, "The game's over! The Mets win the ball game! A line drive to Mario Diaz! They win the damned thing by a score of 10–9!" The always-classy Murphy's use of the word "damn" came across as downright shocking.

Buckner's error. Seaver's almost-perfect game. The year they lost 120 games. The year they won 108. Four trips to the World Series. Two championships. Over the course of more than 6,000 Mets games, Murph saw it all: the good, the bad, the ugly.

LONGEST TENURE BROADCASTING FOR A SINGLE TEAM*

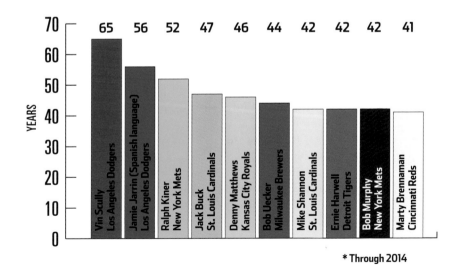

* Through 2014

In 1994, he received the prestigious Ford C. Frick Award in recognition of his broadcasting contributions to baseball and he was inducted into the broadcaster's wing of the National Baseball Hall of Fame in Cooperstown.

"'I am known for ending many broadcasts with the Happy Recap," Murphy told the crowd in Cooperstown on the day of his induction. "This recap is by all odds the happiest of all Happy Recaps."

In 2002, the radio booth at Shea Stadium was the named the Bob Murphy Radio Booth, an honor that transferred over to Citi Field.

Health problems began to affect Murphy's voice and he let it be known that the 2003 season would be his last. On September 26, the Mets had a day for Murphy and every fan in attendance received a VHS tape featuring his best highlight calls. New York City Mayor Michael Bloomberg, singer Julius La Rosa, and Mets great Tom Seaver were on hand to give him a proper sendoff. Among his gifts: a framed No. 42 Mets jersey. Quite a few adults who'd grown up listening to Murphy choked back tears that day, realizing that they were witnessing the end of an era.

Fans were sure they'd heard the last of Murphy after he retired to Florida, until one afternoon in March 2004 when he returned to call one final spring training game. It was such an unexpected treat that fans started calling friends so they, too, could hear that warm, familiar voice again.

Murphy passed away on August 3, 2004, following a brief battle with lung cancer. He was 79. To honor the man whose voice had become synonymous with Mets baseball, the team stitched "Bob Murphy" onto the left sleeve of every player's jersey and wore it for the remainder of the season.

"Bob was a broadcasting icon," said Gary Cohen, who teamed with Murphy on WFAN from 1989 to 2003. "His passion and work ethic were something that every young broadcaster should emulate. It was an honor to work and learn from him."

Reviled Benitez Earns

43

Saves

It's a given that Tug McGraw, Jesse Orosco, John Franco, Randy Myers, and maybe even Skip Lockwood would make a list of the most popular Mets closers ever. Sure to be omitted from such a list would be Armando Benitez, who never won over the Mets faithful but has something that none of those other hurlers have: the club record for most saves in a season with 43, set in 2001.

A big, power-pitching righty from the Dominican Republic, Benitez was acquired from Baltimore for catcher Charles Johnson in December 1998. In his first season in New York, he had 22 saves in 26 opportunities. He served as the setup man for longtime Mets closer John Franco, and when Franco went down with an injury midway through the 1999 season, Benitez assumed the role of full-time closer.

In 2000, despite a painful attack of gout from overindulging in shellfish—you can't make this stuff up—he had 106 strikeouts in

76 innings and successfully closed out 41 games before the Mets embarked on a deep postseason run.

After dropping Game 1 of the NLDS against San Francisco, the Mets held a 2–1 lead entering the ninth inning in Game 2. Edgardo Alfonzo's two-run homer extended the Mets' lead to 4–1. Benitez entered the game with a runner on second after Al Leiter gave up a leadoff double. He promptly allowed a single to Jeff Kent. Two batters later, J.T. Snow stepped to the plate to pinch hit for Ramon Martinez and hit a huge three-run homer that tied the game at 4–4. An RBI single by Jay Payton in the 10th inning put the Mets ahead for good and they went on to win the series.

Then, in Game 1 of the World Series, the Mets held a 3–2 lead over the rival Yankees entering the bottom of the ninth. In came Benitez, who methodically loaded the bases with one out. Yanks second baseman Chuck Knoblauch hit a sacrifice fly into deep left field, scoring Paul O'Neill to tie the game. The Mets went on to lose in the 12th on Jose Vizcaino's RBI single.

Blowing a save against the Reds in April is one thing. Doing it against the Yankees in October was unpardonable. Benitez lost some fans that postseason and never won them back.

The 2001 Mets were below .500 for much of the season. But Benitez was still throwing smoke and his club-record 43 saves were tied for third-most in baseball that year. Benitez was especially sharp in September, when he had nine saves as the Mets went 16–5. But, again, his failures in clutch situations continued to overshadow much of the success he had in his career in New York.

The Mets had won the first two games of a late-season weekend series with the Braves, closing the gap in the NL East to three and a half games. The Mets were primed to finish off the sweep on a Sunday afternoon at Shea, entering the bottom of the ninth up 4–1. Benitez came in to wrap it up, got two outs, then gave up

When the Mets traded Armando Benitez to the Yankees for pitchers Jason Anderson, Anderson Garcia, and Ryan Bicondoa, it was just the 12th trade between the clubs and the first since the Yanks acquired Robin Ventura from the Mets for David Justice on December 7, 2001.

BENITEZ BY THE NUMBERS

Career Saves	**289**
Blown Saves	**59**
Opportunities	**348**
Save percentage	**83%**
Holds	**66**
ERA	**3.13**

a two-run homer to Brian Jordan to cut the lead to 4–3. A walk and two singles later, and the game was tied. New York went on to lose in 11 innings, snapping their five-game winning streak and killing the team's momentum as they hoped to make the postseason for a third straight year.

Even with back-to-back 40-save seasons, which put him in the company of the game's elite closers, Benitez and his propensity for giving up the long ball—39 of the 225 hits he gave up as a Met left the park—had become such a lightning rod for sports-talk radio negativity that it seemed inevitable he would be sent packing...with fans volunteering to drive him to the airport.

That the greatest closer in history was playing over in the Bronx didn't help Benitez's case, either. Whether they were conscious of it or not, some folks just couldn't help measuring him against Mariano Rivera, which was like comparing a Mazda Miata to a Bugatti Veyron. Not really fair.

It's ironic, then, that when the Mets found themselves at 40–53 and sitting in the cellar of the NL East in July 2003, they agreed to trade Benitez to the Yankees, of all teams, to solidify the bridge between their starters and Rivera. It was part of a fire sale that also saw second baseman Roberto Alomar dealt to the Chicago White Sox and outfielder Jeromy Burnitz shipped off to the Los Angeles Dodgers. That the return on Benitez was three non-impact pitchers didn't much matter to the Shea Stadium boo birds, who were generally thrilled just to be rid of him.

A proud, competitive athlete, Armando pitched another five seasons in the majors and even led the league with a career-high 47 saves with Florida in 2004.

New York's First Subway World Series in

44

Years

If nobody outside of the Tri-State area watched a single pitch of the 2000 World Series, that would've been just fine with fans of the Mets and Yankees. For the first time since 1956, when the Yanks beat the Brooklyn Dodgers, New York would be the undisputed center of the baseball universe. As it should be.

The 2000 Mets (94–68) finished just one game behind the division-rival Atlanta Braves, but made the playoffs as the National League wild-card. The Mets knocked off San Francisco in the NLDS and St. Louis in the NLCS. The defending-champion Yankees (87–74) were appearing in their third consecutive World Series.

Thanks to interleague play, introduced three years earlier, some of the novelty had worn off Mets-Yankees games, but this was different. This was David vs. Goliath for all the marbles. The winner wouldn't just be champions of New York, but champions of the world.

The matchups were fascinating, starting at the top with the managers. The brainy but tightly wound Bobby Valentine would match wits with the quietly confident Joe Torre. Bobby V. was a better in-game manager who would rely on stars Mike Piazza, Robin Ventura, and Edgardo Alfonzo, and a solid pitching staff headlined by lefty aces Mike Hampton and Al Leiter. But with the bats of Derek Jeter, Paul O'Neill, Jorge Posada, and Bernie Williams, and the arms of Andy Pettitte, Roger Clemens, and Mariano Rivera, Torre had the superior talent...and the odds. Vegas favored the Yankees, 7–5.

The atmosphere leading up to Game 1, on October 21, was such that, for the first time, the city's beat writers and columnists didn't bother trying to hide which team they were rooting for. Nobody was impartial. Casual fans on both sides became die-hards overnight. Even subway cars on the 4 and 7 lines were decorated in Yankees and Mets colors. If you lived in the area and weren't rooting for one team over the other, you probably didn't have a pulse.

Under the bright lights of Yankee Stadium, postseason veterans Leiter and Pettitte pitched scoreless until the sixth inning when David Justice's two-run double put the Yankees ahead. The Mets rallied to tie in the top of the seventh when Bubba Trammell hit a two-run single off Pettitte, then Alfonzo got an infield hit off middle reliever Jeff Nelson to score Todd Pratt, putting the Mets ahead 3–2. Closer Armando Benitez was on the mound when a sacrifice fly off the bat of Chuck Knoblauch scored Paul O'Neill to tie the game. It was the biggest blown save of Benitez's career. Then, in the 12th inning, ex-Met José Vizcaino got his fourth hit of the night, this one off Turk Wendell, to drive in Tino Martinez to win it for the Yankees.

Game 2, another excruciating loss for the Mets, is memorable for a bizarre scene that played out in the first inning. A pumped-up Clemens was on the mound for the Yankees, and even if he didn't have complete control of his emotions, he seemed to have control of his stuff in striking out the first two batters he faced. Then, up to the plate came Mike Piazza.

These two players had a history that formed one of the many subplots of the World Series. That July, Clemens hit Piazza in the head with a pitch in the second game of a home-and-home doubleheader, knocking the catcher out. He was diagnosed with a concussion and missed the All-Star Game.

Clemens' first pitch to Piazza was a 97-mph fastball. Strike one. Another fastball. Strike two. Then Clemens dealt a splitter for a ball. Piazza swung at the next pitch, a blazing fastball that shattered his bat into three pieces. He still had the handle in his hands while the middle section flew into foul territory off the first-base side and the barrel bounced into the infield, between the mound and first base. Clemens charged off the mound, grabbed the jagged chunk of bat and, to the amazement of everyone watching, angrily hurled it right in the path of Piazza, who was running toward first. Piazza's shock quickly turned to anger. Umpire Charlie Reliford stepped between the players as both dugouts emptied. Somehow, order was restored, play continued, and Piazza grounded out to second. Later, Clemens would claim that he mistook the barrel of the bat for the ball. And if you believe that explanation, we've got a bridge in Queens to sell you.

The 2000 Mets (94–68) finished just one game behind the division rival Atlanta Braves, but made the playoffs as the National League wild-card.

Clemens went on to pitch a brilliant game, allowing just two hits over eight shutout innings, before the Mets roared back with five runs in the ninth courtesy of a two-run blast by Piazza and a three-run shot by Jay Payton. But the Mets' rally was a run short, and they lost 6–5.

The bat-throwing debacle was still the talk of the town as the series shifted to Shea Stadium. The Mets' Game 3 starter, Rick Reed, said that for now, beating the Yankees to win the World Series would be the best revenge. First, though, Reed needed to snap the Bombers'

14-game winning streak in World Series games, a streak dating back to 1996. Reed's career record against the Yanks—0–2 with a 5.26 ERA in five games—did not inspire a lot of confidence.

The game was scoreless in the bottom of the second when Orlando Hernandez threw a fastball high and right over the heart of the plate to Mets fan-favorite Robin Ventura. The third baseman drove the ball to deep right-center, off the base of the scoreboard, to give the Mets a 1–0 lead.

An RBI double by David Justice in the top of the third and an RBI triple by Paul O'Neill in the fourth put the Yanks ahead 2–1. In the

2000 WORLD SERIES LEADERS

Batting Average*

Yankees: Paul O'Neill, .474

Mets: Todd Zeile, .400

*Minimum 10 at-bats

Hits

Yankees: (Tie) Derek Jeter and Paul O'Neill, 9

Mets: Todd Zeile, 8

RBI

Yankees: (Tie) Scott Brosius and David Justice, 3

Mets: Mike Piazza, 4

Walks

Yankees: (Tie) Jorge Posada and Bernie Williams, 5

Mets: Mike Piazza, 4

Strikeouts

Yankees: Derek Jeter, 8

Mets: Benny Agbayani, 6

bottom of the sixth, Todd Zeile hit a line-drive double down the left-field line, scoring Piazza. Tie game.

Rick Reed pitched six strong innings, fanning eight with one walk and two earned runs. Hernandez (12 strikeouts on the night) held the Mets at bay until the bottom of the eighth inning, when Benny Agbayani hit a clutch RBI double to deep left-center. Two batters later, Bubba Trammell hit a sacrifice fly to score pinch runner Joe McEwing. John Franco pitched one inning in relief and was credited

Reed's career record against the Yanks—0–2 with a 5.26 ERA in five games—did not inspire a lot of confidence.

with the win, Benitez earned the save, and the Mets were back in the series.

Jeter, the Yankees' intrepid leadoff man and captain, solidified his case for series MVP in Game 4. On the first pitch of the game, he homered off of Bobby Jones to put the defending champs ahead 1–0. The Yankees added RBI singles in the second and third innings to widen their lead to 3–0. Piazza's two-run blast in the bottom of the third brought the Mets to within a run of tying the game, but they couldn't find a way to solve the Yankees bullpen. Mariano Rivera pitched the final two innings for his sixth career World Series save, tying Rollie Fingers' record. Frustratingly, the Mets lost another one-run game, putting the Yankees just one victory away from completing their three-peat.

The Mets' mantra for Game 5 was "Don't let them celebrate on our field." But in a rematch of the Game 1 starters, Leiter and Pettitte, the Yankees struck first when Bernie Williams hit a second-inning solo home run. The Mets answered with two runs in the bottom of the inning—first when the slow-footed Leiter reached first on a muffed bunt that scored Trammell, and then when Agbayani hit a lazy grounder to third that scored Jay Payton.

Jeter tied the game in the top of the sixth with his second homer of the series. Then, in the ninth inning, with two outs and two men on, utility man Luis Sojo smacked Leiter's 142nd pitch for a two-run single up the middle. That allowed Posada, the go-ahead run, to score, followed by Scott Brosius. The Yanks led 4–2. Franco came in for Leiter and recorded the final out of the inning.

The Mets' last hopes rested on Piazza, who stepped to the plate with a man on and two out against Mariano Rivera. He took Rivera's first pitch for a called strike, then hit the next one hard—hard enough that Shea Stadium's 55,000-plus occupants stopped breathing for a moment, waiting to see if the ball would clear the wall. When it landed in Bernie Williams' glove, just short of the warning track in left-center field, the Yankees poured out of the visitors' dugout to mob Rivera in a scene right out of Mets fans' worst nightmare.

> ... in the 9th inning, with 2 outs and 2 men on, Luis Sojo smacked Leiter's 142nd pitch for a 2-run single up the middle.

Game over. Series over. Dream over.

The 2000 Mets gave their fans one hell of a ride and showed New Yorkers of a certain age how special a Subway World Series could be. That the Yanks' four victories were decided by a total of five runs underscored the importance of making the big play when an opportunity presents itself.

Plays like O'Neill outlasting Benitez in a 10-pitch at-bat before scoring the tying run in Game 1. Or Posada walking on the ninth pitch of his at-bat against an exhausted Leiter in the ninth inning of Game 5, then scoring the go-ahead run.

It still stings.

45

Seasons at Shea

In its infancy, Shea Stadium was criticized by baseball traditionalists for being characterless and antiseptic. In its twilight years, it was still a target of ridicule by fans, opposing players, the press and just about everybody else. As with Nassau Coliseum over in Uniondale, Shea's deterioration was emblematic of an organization clinging to past glories and locked in a cycle of failure and misery.

Ground broke on Shea's eventual replacement, Citi Field, in 2006. Mets fans looked forward to having a new, world-class ballpark, but Shea had been home, *our* home, for 45 years. Whatever its shortcomings, aesthetic or otherwise, it was still the place where Tom Terrific, Kooz, Doc, Darryl, Keith, Gary, and so many other fan favorites gave us a reason to believe that brighter days were ahead. As much as we griped about that blue-and-orange eyesore, we were also sorry to see it go.

Queens was first mentioned as a possible location for a new ballpark sometime after the end of World War II. With the New York Yankees, New York Giants, and Brooklyn Dodgers all battling for supremacy, the city was the center of the baseball universe. Then Dodgers owner Walter O'Malley hatched a plan for a new stadium in Brooklyn to replace Ebbets Field. However, O'Malley couldn't secure land there. City officials offered him a plot out in Queens but O'Malley balked and moved the Dodgers to Los Angeles after the 1957 season. The Giants, too, sought a replacement for the antiquated Polo Grounds in Manhattan, and moved to San Francisco that same off-season.

On October 28, 1961, ground was broken on a new ballpark in Queens.

New York was suddenly a one-ballclub town, but not for long. Mayor Robert Wagner appointed a team of lawyers, led by the tenacious William A. Shea, to acquire a National League franchise for the city. Shea first tried to lure the Reds, Pirates, or Phillies to New York but was unsuccessful. Ultimately, his push to form a Continental League was the strong persuasion Major League Baseball needed to award expansion teams to New York and Houston.

In order for the city to receive an expansion franchise, a new stadium had to be built. On October 28, 1961, ground was broken on a new ballpark in Queens. In the meantime, the Mets had to play in the Polo Grounds for two years while their new stadium was under construction.

It was originally going to be called Flushing Meadow Park Municipal Stadium, the name of the public park—a converted landfill—upon which it was built. But since for most people the word "flushing" conjures images of toilets, concerned citizens successfully lobbied to rename the stadium in honor of the man most directly responsible for bringing baseball to Queens: Bill Shea.

It took 29 months to build and cost between $28.5 to $31 million, depending on the source (by comparison, Citi Field cost a reported $850 million). The first new stadium in the city in more than 40 years boasted unobstructed views and a massive parking lot, amenities that weren't available at Yankee Stadium, Ebbets Field, or the Polo Grounds. Shea was also the first stadium capable of being converted from baseball to football and back using two motor-operated stands that moved on underground tracks. And it had 21 escalators (so fans "won't get a heart attack going to their seats," Casey Stengel bragged) and 54 public restrooms, a lot at the time.

In 1975, while Yankee Stadium was undergoing renovations and the stadium at the Meadowlands was being built, the Mets shared Shea with the Yankees, Jets, and football Giants. It was the first and only time in professional sports history that two baseball teams and two football teams shared the same facility in the same year.

Shea had a long and complicated relationship with the aviation industry. There were times fans and players could barely hear themselves think over the roar of jets taking off from nearby LaGuardia Airport. In fact, sometime during the Mets' inaugural season, an airline pilot purportedly mistook the lights on top of the stadium for La Guardia's runway and nearly hit it as the Mets were taking batting practice before a game against the Cardinals.

On April 17, 1964, in front of 50,312 spectators, the Mets played their first game at Shea, a 4–3 loss to the Pirates. The All-Star Game was played there that season, too, the only time Shea hosted the event. Five years later, the Mets shocked the world by beating Baltimore in the World Series, a feat punctuated by three consecutive home victories. By the 1980s, they were the toast of the town, at last eclipsing the establishment team from the Bronx. Shea, not Yankee Stadium, was the place to be.

A ROCK CATHEDRAL

Shea Stadium was one of the nation's premier concert venues. It figures prominently in the 2010 documentary *Last Play at Shea*, which focuses on Billy Joel's two concerts there in July 2008. A combined 110,000 fans attended the performances, which were also the last held in the stadium before it was torn down. In 1965, Shea hosted the first stateside concert of the Beatles. In 1982, The Clash opened for The Who. And on several occasions, former Police frontman Sting has admitted that the group's 1983 concert at Shea signaled the end of his time with the band because he didn't feel they could get any bigger.

The final game at Shea Stadium, on September 28, 2008, gave all the invisible ghouls who'd taken up residence there one last opportunity to point and snicker at the Mets in their hour of desperation. Even after a heartbreaking 4–2 loss to Florida, which knocked the team out of wild-card contention, Mets fans stayed for a postgame closing ceremony in which a who's who of Mets legends marched onto the field, including Ed Kranepool, Ron Swoboda, Cleon Jones, Dave Kingman, Rusty Staub, Lee Mazzilli, Lenny Dykstra, and Keith Hernandez. Willie Mays, the Say Hey Kid who finished his Hall of Fame career as a Met in 1973, was there, too. The loudest cheers were reserved for Darryl Strawberry and Doc Gooden, one introduced after the other.

Weeks later, demolition crews rolled in to tear down a ballpark which, after only a few years of life, somehow seemed outdated. Today, the parcel on which Shea stood is a parking lot for Citi Field. There's a plaque where home plate used to be, a reminder of memories bitter and sweet.

After the Mets won their second World Series, ownership tried to cash in on the team's popularity by increasing Shea Stadium's seating capacity.

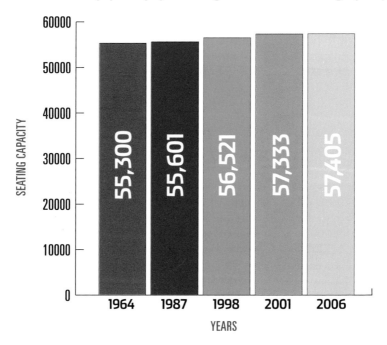

45

Things We'll Never Forget About Shea Stadium

1. The feeling of anticipation as the 7 train pulled into the Shea Stadium/Willets Point stop

2. Old wooden seats eventually replaced with plastic

3. Hot dogs, knishes, and cups of Breyers chocolate and vanilla ice cream

4. Seventh-inning stretch with Lou Monte's "Lazy Mary"

5. Long lines at the restrooms

6. The Diamond Club

7. Green grass, usually perfectly manicured

8. Willie Mays' pink Chrysler Imperial

9. Banner Day double-headers

10. Buckner's error

11. Fan Appreciation Day giveaways

12. The day the stadium shook as if it was going to collapse after Todd Pratt's home run put the Mets into the 1999 NLCS

13. Busted escalators

14. Painting our faces blue and orange for the Subway Series

15. That awful sound system

16. Slipping the usher a few bucks to move to better seats

17. Thursday-afternoon Senior Citizens Day games. Gramps could get in for just 50¢!

18. Showing up early to watch batting practice

19. Meeting Mr. Met

20. Loud vendors throwing bags of peanuts

21. Sipping our first Schaefer or Rheingold

22. Casey, Gil, and Yogi

23. Watching traffic snarl on the Van Wyck

24. The Magic Top Hat and the Home Run Apple

25. 90-foot-tall neon player murals

26. The New York skyline over the center-field scoreboard

27. Cow-Bell Man

28. Mike Piazza's post-9/11 home run

29. Ron Swoboda robbing Brooks Robinson in Game 4 of the 1969 World Series

30. Endy Chavez robbing Scott Rolen in Game 7 of the 2006 NLCS

31. Tom Seaver's "Imperfect Game"

32. Robin Ventura's "Grand Slam Single"

33. Booing Bud Harrelson (as a manager)

34. Booing John Rocker

35. Booing Armando Benitez

36. Booing Chipper Jones

37. "Wait, that's not the same Glenn Close who was in *Fatal Attraction*, is it?"

38. That black cat in front of the Cubs' dugout

39. The ramps

40. The noise

41. The wind

42. The smell

43. The dank

44. Gary Carter jumping onto Jesse Orosco after the final out of the 1986 World Series

45. Chanting "Yankees suck!"

63

Plunks and 0 Regrets for Al Leiter

Over the course of seven Mets seasons, Al Leiter hit 63 batters. It's a franchise record he needn't be ashamed of. Since his fastball didn't blow hitters away—he had an ace's mentality but the arm of a No. 2 starter—Leiter had to find other ways to gain a competitive advantage.

In February 1998, only four months after capturing their first World Series title, the Florida Marlins were still in full-on fire sale mode when they traded Leiter to the Mets for a package of prospects including pitchers A.J. Burnett and Jesus Sanchez and outfielder Rob Stratton.

A 32-year-old native of Toms River, New Jersey, Leiter lost the zip on his fastball due to early arm issues but was successful in Queens because he usually delivered quality starts, kept his team in the game, and was thoroughly unapologetic about his willingness to challenge batters who crowded the plate.

"I don't throw 95 [MPH]," he told *Inside Pitch Magazine*, "so every pitch has a consequence. If I'm going to throw a cutter in on Chipper Jones' hands, I'm going to make sure it's in on Chipper Jones' hands."

It took the cunning lefty a little while to get on a roll in his first Mets campaign, but by early August, Leiter had an 11–4 record. He went on to win 17 games with a 2.47 ERA, both career highs. The team was headed in the right direction and the fans loved their new ace.

> **Leiter went on to win 17 games with a 2.47 ERA, both career highs.**

On the last day of the 1999 regular season, both the Mets and Reds won to finish at 96–66, setting up a wild-card playoff game at old Cinergy Field (Riverfront Stadium) in Cincinnati. Future Hall-of-Famer Rickey Henderson led off with a single. The next batter, Edgardo Alfonzo, homered to give the Mets a 2–0 lead. Leiter did his part, mowing down the Reds en route to a complete-game two-hitter which the Mets won 5–0 win to clinch a wild-card berth.

In Game 4 of the NLDS, Leiter faced Arizona's Brian Anderson and both pitchers delivered quality starts at Shea Stadium. The Mets eventually won the game on a miracle home run off the bat of Todd Pratt to advance to the NLCS. In that series, Leiter dueled future-Met Tom Glavine and the division-champ Atlanta Braves. Each hurler lasted seven innings but the Mets lost 1–0. Leiter started Game 6 on fumes and just three days' rest. He never made it out of the first inning, giving up five runs. The Mets lost the game and the series but Leiter and company had renewed hopes heading into the new millennium.

DID YOU KNOW? Al Leiter ranks 53rd all-time in hit batsmen with 117, well behind the leader in that category, August "Gus" Weyhing. A righty who pitched for nine teams in a career that spanned 14 years from 1887 to 1901, Wehing hit 277 batters.

AL LEITER: HIT BATTERS BY SEASON

Year	Hit Batters
1987	0
1988	5
1989	2
1990	0
1991	0
1992	0
1993	4
1994	2
1995	6
1996	11
1997	9
1998	11
1999	9
2000	11
2001	4
2002	8
2003	9
2004	11
2005	12

Leiter was still the ace of the staff in 2000, as well as an important team leader and spokesman, when he won 16 games and was named an All-Star for the second time in his career. With playoff wins over the Giants and Cardinals, he helped the Mets get to their first World Series in 14 years. He would face the team that drafted him 50th overall in 1984: the Yankees.

Here was the opportunity of a lifetime for a pitcher who had won some huge games for the Mets but who also had endured a string of bad luck in the postseason, dating back to his years with the Blue Jays and Marlins. Leiter had lost all seven of his previous playoff starts, his only win in October coming with Toronto in 1993, and that was in relief.

Manager Bobby Valentine's decision to go with Leiter over Mike Hampton in Game 1 of the Fall Classic raised some eyebrows, if only because Hampton had just been named Most Valuable Player of the NLCS. But Leiter had more playoff experience than anyone on the Mets staff and was, Valentine assumed, due for a win.

Even if Leiter claimed to have no hard feelings for his former team, his body language on the mound suggested otherwise. Dominant in Game 1—the longest World Series game in history up to that point at four hours and 51 minutes—he struck out seven over six

Al Leiter puts a champagne-filled hat on Bobby V.'s head after Leiter pitched a two-hit shutout to beat the Reds 5–0 in the 1999 NL wild-card tie-breaker game. *(David Kohl via AP Images)*

strong innings. Unfortunately, he then watched his bullpen blow a 3–2 lead and lose in extra innings.

Game 5 featured a rematch of the two lefties who started the series, Leiter and Andy Pettitte. With the Yankees just one win away from their third consecutive championship, Leiter struck out nine in a valiant bid to extend the Mets' season. The score was tied 2–2 at the top of the ninth inning when he threw his 142nd and final pitch of the night to utility man Luis Sojo, who drove in two runs with a grounder to center field. Valentine, who'd gambled that his starter still had enough in the tank to go the distance, finally pulled Leiter out and sent in John Franco. Al walked gloomily to the dugout where TV cameras captured the pitcher slumped over with his head buried in his hands.

Although the Mets never reached the playoffs again during Leiter's time with the club, he continued to be a tough competitor well into his late thirties. After the 2004 season, he hoped to sign a one-year deal to stay with the Mets and then likely call it a career. But first-year GM Omar Minaya badly bungled contract talks with the pitcher, who accepted an offer to stay in New York only to see that offer rescinded a few days later. Angry and hurt, Leiter signed a one-year deal with the Marlins.

Dominant in Game 1...
Leiter **struck out 7**
over six strong innings.

It certainly wasn't the first time a popular Met left town in a huff. New York fans were generally savvy enough to know not to take it personally, especially since Al had been vocal about wanting to retire as a Met and placed the blame for the breakdown in negotiations squarely on Minaya.

From his earliest guest appearances on WFAN's *Mike and the Mad Dog,* it was clear Leiter grasped the subtle nuances of baseball and that he was destined for a post-playing career in broadcasting. He has worked as a color commentator and a studio analyst for the YES Network and MLB Network.

Despite

82

Wins, "Ya Gotta Believe!"

The 1973 Mets won the weak NL East Division with a record of 82–79 before shocking the world by making it to Game 7 of the World Series. Anyone who didn't believe the team could go that far clearly hadn't been in the company of one Frank Edwin "Tug" McGraw.

New York's .509 winning percentage that season was the lowest of any pennant winner in major league history until 2005, when the San Diego Padres won the awful NL West with a winning percentage of .506 (82–80). From May to July, the Mets lost 49 games and won only 32. By Independence Day, they found themselves 12½ games behind the first-place Chicago Cubs.

Managed by Yogi Berra, the '73 Mets didn't set any offensive records—not with right fielder Rusty Staub (15 home runs, 36 doubles, 76 RBI, .279 batting average), John "The Hammer" Milner (career-high 23 homers, 72 RBI), and third baseman Wayne Garrett (16 homers) leading the way. The club was in the bottom third of every offensive statistic in the National League, except for walks, where they had the sixth-best rate in the league.

The only thing the Mets really had going for them was pitching: righty Tom Seaver (19 wins, 2.08 ERA) and lefties Jerry Koosman, Jon Matlack, and George Stone. As a team, the Mets led the league in strikeouts (1,027), were third in the league with a 3.26 ERA, and allowed the second-fewest hits (1,345).

> ...the Mets caught fire and never cooled off, closing out the season on a **49–22** run.

Even with all those great arms, there really was no reason to believe the last-place Mets could overtake Chicago to make the playoffs, let alone the World Series. But Tug McGraw, New York's lefty reliever, believed. Or at least he pretended he did. After team chairman M. Donald Grant delivered one of his eye-roll-inducing pep talks during a team meeting, assuring players that he still believed in them, McGrew ran around the locker room sarcastically asking teammates "Do you believe? Do you believe? Ya gotta believe!"

What started as a joke during a slump became the stuff of legend. In August, the Mets caught fire and never cooled off, closing out the season on a 49–22 run. The Cubs went into a tailspin and never recovered. You might say the Mets stole the NL East crown, but the Cubs left it sitting on an open windowsill.

The Mets rolled into Wrigley Field on October 1, 1973, and on a chilly and damp afternoon in front of just 1,913 fans, the visitors overcame a shaky start by Seaver to beat the Cubs 6–4 and clinch the pennant.

Perhaps the most memorable moment of that postseason occurred in Game 3 of the NLCS, a Monday afternoon in Queens. Though everyone expected Cincinnati's "Big Red Machine" to steamroll New York, they split the first two games of the series. But steamroll is exactly what 200-pound All-Star Pete Rose appeared to do to Bud Harrelson, barreling into the Mets' 146-pound shortstop to break up a double play. Words were exchanged, Rose pushed Harrelson to the ground, and both dugouts emptied. In the brawl that ensued, the Reds' Pedro Borbon and New York's Buzz Capra exchanged punches.

A short time later, when Rose took his spot in left field, fans showered him with beer cans, batteries, and whatever else they could get their hands on. When a whiskey bottle flew past Rose, manager Sparky Anderson called his team off the field. A group of Mets players, joined by Berra, went out to left field to calm the natives and remind them that even though New York led 9–2, they could still forfeit the game. The crowd settled down after that, though police filled into the section to make sure there were no more flare-ups.

The Reds staved off elimination in Game 4, winning 2–1.

In the decisive fifth game, the Mets scored four runs in the fifth en route to a 7–2 victory. Seaver struck out four and allowed one run over eight-plus innings. McGraw, who had quieted the Reds' bats by not allowing a run in two games, got the save.

The prospect of seeing their team in the World Series for the second time in four years was just too much for Mets fans to handle—so much so that thousands in the crowd of 50,000-plus stormed the field of Shea Stadium, delaying the game in the ninth inning so they could claw huge chunks of sod, fencing, and fixtures from the park. Maybe they couldn't believe their eyes and needed tangible proof that what they were witnessing wasn't a dream. Poor Willie Mays, making his first appearance in a month, and other players very nearly ended up as mementos themselves. Strangers grabbed at their uniforms. Hundreds of police officers were needed to restore order.

It took a little while for Mets fans to warm to George Stone. Early in the 1972 season, while pitching for the Braves, Stone plunked Rusty Staub on the wrist, fracturing it. But then he was dealt to the Mets for pitchers Danny Frisella and the popular Gary Gentry. After a short stint in the bullpen, Stone was moved into the rotation, and in 1973 he posted a 12–3 record as New York's No. 4 starter.

Repairs on the stadium started immediately after the game, when the last of the frenzied fans had been sent off to continue their revelry elsewhere. The Mets celebrated their victory with champagne and prepared to meet the winner of the ALCS: the Baltimore Orioles or the defending champs from Oakland.

The A's were a virtual All-Star team with big names at every position. The Mets had superior pitching but aside from Rusty Staub, their hitting was weak. When he ran into a fence in the NLCS, separating his shoulder, it didn't affect his bat but he would be forced to throw underhand when he was able to play.

Staub missed the series opener in Oakland, in which the A's scored a pair of unearned runs in the third inning off Matlack. That was all they'd need, as lefty Ken Holtzman and a pair of relievers limited the Mets to a single run. It was Willie Mays' last major league start. Once the most graceful outfielder to ever set foot on a baseball diamond, Mays on that day looked every one of his 42 years, falling down trying to make a play with the world watching. The normally sure-gloved second baseman, Felix Millan, also had a ground ball go through his legs. The highlight of that game for Mets fans might have been seeing Jim Nabors (television's Gomer Pyle) singing the National Anthem.

Game 2 was a wild affair, as Oakland scored two runs in the ninth to force extra innings, only to lose 10–7 when the Mets scored four times in the top of the 12th. All four of those runs were unearned because of a pair of errors by A's second baseman Mike Andrews. The Mets used five pitchers in the game and McGraw was credited with the win.

A's owner Charley Finley was fuming over Andrews' gaffes. Prior to Game 3, Finley tried to get his second baseman removed from the roster, claiming he had a shoulder injury. Baseball commissioner Bowie Kuhn saw through Finley's deception and ordered Andrews reinstated. Kuhn also fined Finley $11,000 and placed him on probation.

Game 3 in New York featured a matchup of the NL's Cy Young winner, Seaver, versus Jim "Catfish" Hunter, who'd finished third in AL Cy Young voting. Garrett's first inning homer put the Mets ahead 1–0. Hunter lasted six while Seaver lasted eight, striking

1973: A TALE OF TWO HALVES

Split	W	L	RS	RA	WP
First Half	42	51	348	377	.452
Second Half	40	28	260	211	.588

out 12 with two earned runs. In the top of the eighth, Oakland's Joe Rudi knotted the game at 2–2 with an RBI single. In the 11th, Bert Campaneris singled to center off Mets reliever Harry Parker, scoring Ted Kubiak to give the A's a 3–2 win.

Oakland's bats went quiet in Games 4 and 5, the Mets winning 6–1 and 2–0, with Koosman and McGraw combining for the fifth-game shutout.

Facing elimination in Game 6, the A's came through with a 3–1 victory behind solid pitching from Catfish Hunter and a pair of RBI doubles from Reggie Jackson.

Game 7 was all Oakland, as the A's went up 4–0 in the third when Campaneris and Jackson both blasted two-run homers off Game 4 winner Jon Matlack. They tacked on another in the fifth when Joe Rudi's single drove in Campaneris. The Mets scored a run in the sixth and another in the ninth, but with two runners on base, Darold Knowles retired Garrett on a pop-up to shortstop to end the game, giving the A's their second straight World Series.

It was an autumn full of drama and controversy, aging stars and meddling owners. The sting of the loss was still fresh in the Mets locker room, but among players like Staub, there was also an overwhelming feeling of pride.

"It's really something to be proud of," Staub said. "For me personally, I'd never in my whole life been a part of anything like this. To be able to come back from last place in our division, like we did, then win the playoff and get to the seventh game, I'm really proud of what we did."

90

Percent of the Game is Mental. The Other Half is Physical.

Yogi Berra is certainly more famous for his fractured English and sometimes nonsensical quotes than for the three-plus seasons he spent as manager of the Mets. Some famous Yogiisms include:

"If the world were perfect, it wouldn't be."

"It ain't the heat, it's the humility."

"Ninety percent of the game is mental. The other half is physical."

"A home opener is always exciting, no matter if it's home or on the road."

And it was Yogi who said of the 1973 pennant race, "It ain't over til it's over." And he was right!

Speaking to *The Saratogian*, pitcher Jon Matlack shared fond memories of that season and of playing for Yogi, though it was sometimes difficult to understand Berra when he'd come out to the mound. Exasperated, Matlack finally turned to teammate Tom Seaver for help.

"It's real easy," Seaver said. "When Yogi comes out to the mound and says whatever he says, if he doesn't put his hand out, just say okay. He'll go back to the dugout. If he puts his hand out, put the ball in it and you go back to the dugout. It's that simple."

Matlack thrived under Berra's managerial style.

"Yogi was a gem," he said. "Yogi would not over-manage. By today's standards he would under-manage. It was, 'Let's put the right people on the field and let them play the game. Maybe we'll make a change here or there.' He was very easy to play for and work with."

Lawrence Peter Berra—the nickname "Yogi" was inspired by his habit of sitting cross-legged like a yogi—won a record 10 World Series titles with the Yankees.

Berra was hired by the Mets in November 1964 to work as a coach under manager Casey Stengel. The men knew each other well from their time together with the Yankees. At the time, the idea was for the 39-year-old former catcher to get in shape during spring training to see if he could be a player/coach and pinch hitter (Berra batted .285 with 358 home runs before hanging up his cleats the previous autumn).

At a huge press conference at Shea Stadium, both Berra and George Weiss, president of the Mets and former general manager of the Yankees, said there was no agreement in place for Berra to eventually succeed Stengel. However, they had a handshake agreement that if a managerial job opened up someplace else, Yogi would be free to pursue it.

On May 1, 1965, Berra made his Mets debut as a player when he came up as a pinch hitter for reliever Jim Bethke in the eighth inning of a 9–2 loss to Cincinnati. He grounded out.

Three days later, against the Phillies, he had two singles in a 2–1 Mets win. Those would be the last hits of his Hall of Fame career, bringing the total to a tidy 2,150 over 2,120 major league games. In that same game, one of only four he ever played as a Met, he also scored the winning run in the seventh inning.

Unfortunate circumstances created a managerial opening with the Mets on April 2, 1972, when Stengel's successor, Gil Hodges, suffered a fatal heart attack following a round of golf in Palm Beach, Florida. With Opening Day less than two weeks away, the team had to fill the post quickly. The Mets hierarchy of team owner Joan Payson and chairman M. Donald Grant were harshly criticized in the press for introducing Berra as the new manager on the same day Hodges was laid to rest. The timing was awful.

It was an impossibly awkward situation for Yogi, who tried to say all the right things in accepting the promotion when such a somber mood hovered over the club. He knew he had big shoes to fill, and gave Hodges all the credit for having prepared the team during spring training.

Deep down, Yogi was eager to show the baseball world that the pennant he'd won in 1964 as manager of the Yankees hadn't been a fluke.

The club got off to a hot start, playing better than .700 ball in early June. But soon after, a series of injuries sidelined key players like Bud Harrelson, Jerry Grote, Cleon Jones, and new slugger Rusty Staub. The Mets finished 10 games over .500 but dropped to third place in the division for the third consecutive season.

YOGI'S METS

Year	Record	Percent	Games	Finish
1972	83–73	.532	156	Third
1973	82–79	.509	161	First
1974	71–91	.438	162	Fifth
1975	56–53	.514	109*	Third

* Replaced mid-season

A bad first half of the 1973 season led to rumors that Berra's job was in jeopardy. A fan poll conducted by the *New York Post* showed that a majority considered Yogi least responsible for the team's troubles and actually preferred seeing general manager Bob Scheffing get the ax. But then, in late August, the Mets' fortunes turned and they finished strong enough to win the division. After clipping the Cincinnati Reds in the NLDS, New York reached the World Series and had a 3–2 lead going into Game 6 in Oakland.

Yogi passed over the rested George Stone and gave the ball to his ace, Seaver, to pitch on three days' rest. Seaver went seven, yielding just two runs while striking out six, but was outdueled

> *The club got off to a hot start, playing better than* **.700 ball** *in early June.*

by Catfish Hunter in a 3–1 loss. When the Mets lost Game 7, 5–2, Berra shouldered more of the blame than he should have because he'd chosen to skip Stone a second time to start Matlack on three days' rest.

Berra remained popular up until his abrupt firing in August 1975. After suspending Cleon Jones for not reporting to the outfield during a game in which he had already pinch-hit, Berra refused management's order to reinstate him. A defiant Yogi told the team that either he or Jones had to go. In the end, they were both out of a job.

Ninety percent of the time, Berra was a lovable, easygoing character. The other half of the time? Watch out.

Overworked Feliciano Takes the Mound

92

Times

Pedro Feliciano is living proof that you really can have too much of a good thing. The lefty reliever nicknamed "Perpetual Pedro" was so overused during his time with the Mets that his body eventually broke down. But those critical of the Mets for allowing Feliciano to set franchise records for appearances three straight years (86, 88, and 92 games) sometimes overlook the fact that he always wanted the ball. Pedro would've taken the mound 100 times if they'd let him.

Feliciano was drafted in the 31st round back in 1995 by the Los Angeles Dodgers. A shoulder injury set him back and he pitched for six more years in the minors. When he became a free agent he signed with the Cincinnati Reds in 2002. That August he was traded to the Mets. He looked good early but then floundered and was returned to the minors.

In 2005, he left for greener pastures in the Land of the Rising Sun and had some success playing for the Fukuoka SoftBank Hawks. The Mets took notice and brought Feliciano back for the 2006 season. He appeared in 64 games for New York, a heavier workload compared to the 51 games he pitched over his first three major league seasons.

The Mets made the playoffs and Feliciano provided another trusted arm in the pen. He pitched in all three games of the 2006 NLDS as New York swept the Dodgers. He didn't allow a hit or a run. It seemed like Feliciano might pitch in every Mets playoff game.

The NLCS versus the Cardinals, a seesaw battle that went seven games, saw Mets manager Willie Randolph turn to Feliciano three more times—but not in Game 7, when the tall righty Aaron Heilman surrendered a two-run homer to Yadier Molina.

*Pedro Feliciano's **344** appearances from 2007 to 2010 is a major league record.*

Trailing 3–1, the Mets loaded the bases in the bottom of the inning, but Carlos Beltran struck out looking.

Many fans thought Feliciano should have been used over Heilman, who got the loss. It was the last playoff game ever at Shea Stadium, and the beginning of a lengthy postseason draught. On the plus side, the rubber-armed Feliciano had established himself as an important and popular presence on the Mets' pitching staff.

For the next three seasons, the lefty specialist put up staggering numbers while the Mets continued to break their fans' hearts with late-season collapses. In 2007, he appeared in 78 games. In 2008, he took the hill 86 times. The following season, 88. And in 2010, he made an incredible 92 relief appearances. Although the Dodgers' Mike Marshall holds the single-season record with 106 relief appearances, set in 1974, Feliciano's 344 appearances from 2007 to 2010 is also a major league record. He had no equal during that span, even passing the legendary Tom Seaver on the club list for games pitched.

Feliciano wouldn't have been given the ball that often if his numbers weren't good. But after 2010, there was growing concern about his workload. Over a five-year span, he'd already pitched in a staggering 408 games. Even during the busiest four-year stretch of his career, Marshall only pitched in 387 games.

Pedro Feliciano in one of his 92 appearances in 2010. *(G. Fiume)*

In January 2011, Feliciano left the Mets to sign a two-year deal with the Yankees. He never pitched for them. In spring training, Feliciano developed pain in his left shoulder, was found to have a torn rotator cuff and was shut down for the season. Yankees GM Brian Cashman slammed the Mets for overusing Feliciano, going so far as saying the number of times Feliciano had pitched over the years amounted to abuse. When he became a free agent in 2012, the Yankees let him walk.

With $8 million of the Steinbrenners' money in his pocket, Feliciano signed a minor league deal with the only major league team for which he'd ever played: the Mets. He eventually worked his way back to Queens and pitched 25 games during the 2013 season. Feliciano's 484 games pitched for the Mets is second all-time behind John Franco's 695.

Over a **5-year span** *Feliciano pitched a staggering* **408 games.**

Piersall's

100th

Career Home Run

Outfielder Jimmy Piersall played 17 years of major league ball with five teams, batting .272 with 104 home runs. As colorful a personality as the game has ever seen, Piersall made sure that homer No. 100 was his most memorable. He marked the occasion by running the bases backwards.

A product of Waterbury, Connecticut, Jimmy became a local legend at 14, playing in a league featuring men twice his age. He was a three-sport star in high school who led his basketball team to three straight New England championship finals.

Signing with the Boston Red Sox after high school, he made his major league debut two years later. The more he played, the more that people began to notice in him some peculiar behaviors. He seemed to delight in provoking opposing players, fans, and umpires, and was known to take a bow after every catch. No one knew it at the time, but Piersall's personality quirks were actually early signs of mental illness.

He eventually sought treatment for manic depression—what we know today as bipolar disorder—and spent time in a psychiatric hospital. His successful return to baseball after missing most of the 1952 season remains one of the great comeback stories the game has ever seen.

Despite finishing third in the American League in batting with a career-high .322 average and winning his second Gold Glove while playing for the Cleveland Indians in 1961, Piersall was traded to Washington. He spent parts of two seasons with the Senators before being dealt in 1963 to the Mets for Gil Hodges, who then became Washington's manager.

Although over a decade removed from his hospitalization, Jimmy was still something of a wild-card by the time he arrived in New York, as noted by his manager, Casey Stengel.

"He's great," Stengel said, "but you have to play him in a cage."

Actually, Piersall had been known as one of the game's top fielders, making up for his lack of quickness with excellent anticipation. A two-time All-Star, he won two Gold Gloves as a center fielder (1958, 1961). His .990 lifetime fielding percentage ranks among the highest all-time.

"I thought Joe DiMaggio was the greatest defensive outfielder I ever saw," said Stengel, who managed DiMaggio from 1949 to 1951. "But I have to rate Piersall better."

As a Met, Piersall was still sharp defensively, but he struggled at the plate, batting a career-worst .194 with an awful .516 OPS in 40 games. That helps explain why his brief stay in New York is remembered for one reason: he ran the bases backward after hitting his 100th career home run on June 23, 1963.

DID YOU KNOW? Jimmy Piersall's rise to baseball stardom and battle with mental illness was dramatized in the 1957 film *Fear Strikes Out*, starring Anthony Perkins (*Psycho*). The movie was based on a book of the same title written by Piersall and Al Hirshberg.

It happened in the first game of a doubleheader against the Philadelphia Phillies at the Polo Grounds. The Mets had a 1–0 lead in the bottom of the fifth when Piersall drove a pitch from Dallas Green over the right-field fence. As perplexed Philadelphia players looked on, Piersall backpedaled around the bases, making sure to touch each base in correct order. Along the way, he shook hands with the third base coach.

Supposedly, the stunt was all part of a plan Piersall hatched earlier in the season when he saw how little fanfare teammate Duke Snider received for hitting his 400th career home run. Jimmy was determined to get more publicity with his 100th than Snider did with his 400th. At that, he was successful. But Piersall's first quadruple as a Met would also be his last.

POWER OUTAGE IN QUEENS

As a team, the 1963 Mets hit only 96 home runs:

Jim Hickman	17
Frank Thomas	15
Duke Snider	14
Tim Harkness	10
Ron Hunt	10
Joe Hicks	5
Choo-Choo Coleman	3
Charlie Neal	3
Duke Carmel	3
Jesse Gonder	3
Ed Kranepool	2
Norm Sherry	2
Cliff Cook	2
Jimmy Piersall	1*

*Six others tied with 1

Mets fans didn't have a lot to smile about in 1963, as their team would lose 111 games and finish in last place in the National League. To them, Piersall's theatrics provided a much-needed moment of levity. Stengel was not amused, however, and cut the veteran outfielder two days later.

Piersall rediscovered his swing with the Angels, retiring as a member of that club in 1967. He went on to enjoy an extremely eventful second life in baseball, most notably as one of the game's most outspoken broadcasters.

Nolan Ryan Walks

116

Batters

The Mets' decision to trade Nolan Ryan in 1971, the same season he walked a club-record 116 batters, has been called one of the biggest blunders in baseball history. Certainly, it was torture to watch Ryan rise to stardom wearing another team's laundry. But, in their defense, the Mets didn't know they were giving up on a future Hall-of-Famer who would retire as baseball's all-time strikeout leader.

Although he was a contributor on the Mets' first world championship in 1969 and threw harder than anybody else on the staff, including Tom Seaver, Ryan always had control issues. Because of his erratic performances, he bounced back and forth from the starting rotation to the bullpen and never really found a role in Flushing. That didn't help the young Texan to get comfortable in the Big Apple, even though he had Seaver—a team leader and clubhouse cut-up—as a roommate. Ryan's bullpen coach, Joe Pignatano, sensed Nolan wouldn't be with the Mets for very long.

"How long can you wait?" Mets general manager Bob Scheffing said of Nolan Ryan after trading the fireballer in 1971. *(Louis Requena)*

A 12th-round draft pick of the Mets in 1965, Ryan made his major league debut a year later on September 11, 1966, in relief against the Atlanta Braves. In that game, he registered his first strikeout (against Pat Jarvis) and surrendered his first home run (to future Mets player and manager Joe Torre).

Ryan missed much of the 1967 season due to illness, an arm injury, and service with the Army Reserve, pitching only seven innings for the Mets' minor league affiliate in Jacksonville. He did not stick in the majors for good until the 1968 season. Even with a fastball often exceeding 100 MPH, he was unable to crack the Mets' deep starting rotation led by Seaver and Jerry Koosman. Ryan was used more as a reliever and spot starter by the 1969 Mets. He pitched well that postseason, most notably helping the Mets complete their sweep of Atlanta in the NLCS by throwing seven innings to win Game 3. In the World Series against Baltimore, he pitched two scoreless innings in Game 3 and got the save.

On April 18, 1970, Ryan tied a Mets record by striking out 15 batters in one game. Just a few days later, Seaver topped it with 19 against the San Diego Padres. Ryan has credited his time with Seaver and the Mets with helping him evolve from someone who just threw hard into a real major league pitcher.

In 1971, Ryan's fifth season in the majors, he started 26 games—a substantial workload for a pitcher who, up to that point, hadn't earned the complete trust of his manager and coaches. He went

ALL-TIME LEADERS: INNINGS PITCHED

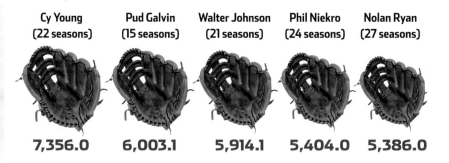

Cy Young (22 seasons)	Pud Galvin (15 seasons)	Walter Johnson (21 seasons)	Phil Niekro (24 seasons)	Nolan Ryan (27 seasons)
7,356.0	6,003.1	5,914.1	5,404.0	5,386.0

10–14 with a 3.97 ERA, allowing 125 hits over 152 innings. His 116 walks allowed is a club mark that has held up for over 40 years.

The Mets lost their patience with the 24-year-old power pitcher, and on December 10, traded him with catcher Frank Estrada, pitcher Don Rose, and outfielder Leroy Stanton to the California Angels for veteran shortstop/third baseman Jim Fregosi. A former All-Star in decline, Fregosi would play parts of just two seasons in New York before being dealt to the Texas Rangers.

And Ryan? In his first season as an Angel, he won 19 games, played in his first All-Star Game, and recorded a MLB-leading 329 strikeouts. He also led the league with 157 walks. This would become a common theme throughout Nolan's amazing 27-year career. He retired in 1993 at age 46 with the seemingly unbreakable records of 5,714 strikeouts *and* 2,795 walks. He also still holds the major league marks for hits allowed per nine innings pitched with 6.6 and most career no-hitters with seven.

In hindsight, yes, it was one of the worst trades ever. But there weren't many complaints at the time. Nolan wasn't "The Ryan Express" just yet and the Mets needed a third baseman.

"I really can't say I quit on him," Mets general manager Bob Scheffing said of Ryan shortly after completing the deal. "But we've had him three full years and, although he's a hell of a prospect, he hasn't done it for us. How long can you wait? I can't rate him in the same category with Tom Seaver, Jerry Koosman, or Gary Gentry."

ALL-TIME LEADERS: WILD PITCHES

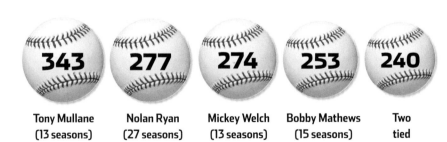

343	277	274	253	240
Tony Mullane (13 seasons)	Nolan Ryan (27 seasons)	Mickey Welch (13 seasons)	Bobby Mathews (15 seasons)	Two tied

deGrom Strikes Out

144

and Wins Rookie of the Year

What a whirlwind season 2014 was for Jacob deGrom. The lanky, 26-year-old Floridian with the Grunge-era locks began the year with Triple-A Las Vegas and ended it as the 2014 National League Rookie of the Year by battling his way into the Mets' rotation, going 9–6 with a 2.69 ERA in 22 starts, and striking out 144 batters over $140^{1}/_{3}$ innings.

deGrom was the fifth Met to win the award, following Tom Seaver (1967), Jon Matlack (1972), Darryl Strawberry (1983), and Dwight Gooden (1984). He beat out the likes of Reds center fielder Billy Hamilton and Cardinals second baseman Kolten Wong. deGrom won with 26 of 30 first-place votes.

The modern era of professional baseball is a battlefield for pitchers. They're expected to throw their hardest on every pitch to every batter. The position has completely changed from the old days, when hurlers paced themselves so they could last to the later innings. Today's pitchers are developing major arm injuries earlier in their careers and deGrom was no exception.

He has a 90-plus MPH fastball, but he was drafted in the ninth round of the 2010 draft because he was a shortstop/pitcher in college. The Mets envisioned him as a full-time pitcher. Others have made the transition successfully in the past, but there's always an element of risk involved. The risk was heightened with deGrom because he underwent Tommy John surgery and missed all of 2011 recovering.

There was little buzz about deGrom in spring training and he didn't make the Opening Day roster. The Mets sent him down to minor league camp. Another pitcher would've sulked over that but he decided to make the most of it. On May 12, 2014, he got the big league call when he was scratched from his intended start for the Las Vegas 51s, the Mets' Triple-A club with which he'd amassed a 4–0 record.

On May 15, he earned his first major league start against the crosstown rival Yankees. He pitched a tidy seven innings, giving up just one run and striking out six in a 1–0 loss. In that game, he got his first hit in his first at-bat, becoming the first Mets pitcher to get a hit in the 2014 season. Up to that point, the staff was a

METS PITCHERS Ks PER INNING

Pitcher	IP	SO	Ks per inning
Jacob deGrom	140.1	144	1.02
Zack Wheeler	185.1	187	1.01
Bartolo Colon	202.1	151	.74
Jon Niese	187.2	138	.73
Dillon Gee	137.1	94	.68

Jacob deGrom on his way to capturing the 2014 NL Rookie of the Year Award. *(Otto Greule Jr)*

collective 0-for-64, setting a major league record for futility at the plate to start a season.

Jacob endured his own little stretch of futility by being the first Mets pitcher to go winless in his first seven starts. On June 21, he picked up his first career win after pitching seven scoreless innings against the Marlins.

On July 8, deGrom pitched another seven scoreless innings ... the 4,000th win in Mets history.

On July 8, deGrom pitched another seven scoreless innings against the Braves to achieve a franchise milestone: the 4,000th win in Mets history. The phenom struck out 11 batters in an 8–3 Mets victory. It was his second 11-strikeout performance in his first 11 starts, a feat previously accomplished only by Nolan Ryan and Dwight Gooden.

A lot of pitchers make their major league debuts while still in their early twenties. There's no reason to believe that deGrom, who didn't hit the scene until he was 26 but arrived with a healthy arm and plenty of confidence, won't be an important piece of the Mets' plans for many years to come.

145

Whiffs: Mo Vaughn Strikes Out as a Met

Many Met fans will remember the name Mo Vaughn. The burly first baseman was an all-star caliber first baseman for the Boston Red Sox. In 1996, he hit 44 round trippers, drove in 143, and hit .326. Just two years later he signed in Anaheim as a free agent, and by 2001 he was out of baseball because of injury.

In late December 2001 the Mets traded overpriced and aging starter Kevin Appier to the Anaheim Angels for Vaughn and his reported $12.1 million salary, which would escalate to $17.1 million for the next two seasons. It was a risk, and most fans asked what kind of shape the reported 225-pounder was in and could he return to form?

Mets GM Steve Phillips and manager Bobby Valentine visited the "Hit Dog Training Center" that Vaughn owned, saw the Norwalk, Connecticut, native hit, and decided to trade for a guy who missed an entire season with a biceps injury. It was risky, but the Mets lost out on signing slugger Juan Gonzalez, so they were desperate.

At 34, Vaughn wasn't considered over the hill, but he was looked at as an out-of-shape athlete who wouldn't have a long career due to the extra weight he would carry each season. Some fans worried about this, others liked the signing.

In January 2002, Vaughn proclaimed his strip-club days were over in a *New York Post* article. He was 270 pounds at the time but was hoping to lose 10 pounds by Valentine's Day. He had dreamt about the Mets. It all sounded too good to be true.

Vaughn reported to training camp at 268 pounds. He couldn't hide and his slow start made him a laughing stock on local sports talk radio and in every newspaper. At the end of April Vaughn had just 1 home run. The hopes of fans in that 2002 season were fading fast.

With a new commitment to fitness, the Mets slugger, now 35, thought he could play five more years.

By the end of May he had four homers. At that point it was pretty clear he wasn't the same player. He did get "hot" and hit 26 homers, drove in 72, and hit a paltry .259. He struck out 145 times, setting a Mets record for a left-handed hitter. The Mets ended the season at 75–86 in fifth place. This was turning into a disaster.

In the off-season, Met fans started to hear about the Foxy Lady strip club in Providence, Rhode Island, again. Red Sox fans knew it well when Vaughn had a scrape with the law there in 1998. He got an early morning DUI, failed eight sobriety tests, and couldn't recite the alphabet past the letter "P" three times, plus he crashed his car into an abandoned vehicle on a highway service lane.

A "slimmer" Mo Vaughn reported to training camp in 2003 with high hopes. He arrived to training camp in Port St. Lucie in a black stretch limo, and when he exited the vehicle, the photographers and gaggle of reporters liked what they saw. Vaughn wouldn't discuss his actual weight but instead chose to talk about his diet.

With a new commitment to fitness, the Mets slugger, now 35, thought he could play five more years.

That optimism wouldn't last. Vaughn complained early on about knee pain and after just 27 games his season was over. The knee was first reported as "arthritic," but then reports changed. In January of 2004, he was proclaimed to be out for the entire next season. He never got surgery because he had no cartilage and felt he was too young for a knee replacement. This saga about his knee dragged on long enough for the Mets to recoup a fair amount of his contract due to an insurance policy they had purchased on the then-275-pound player.

Vaughn hit a total of 29 home runs as a Met. A few were tape-measure shots, but not enough to win over the critics. Fans would continue to blame Phillips for signing him and he was fired in June of 2003. He had a nice run, but the signing of Vaughn was the straw that broke the camel's back.

In December of 2007 it was revealed that Vaughn had purchased human growth hormone from Mets clubhouse employee Kirk Radomski, as mentioned in the infamous Mitchell Report.

Dave Kingman's

156

Strikeouts

Babe Ruth once said, "Never let the fear of striking out get in your way." It's as much a life lesson as a baseball lesson. Dave Kingman, one of the most talked about sluggers of his era, wasn't afraid to strike out (and if he was, he didn't show it). A 6'6", 210-pound specimen of a man with freakishly long arms, he could launch moon shots when his bat connected with the ball. And when it didn't, well, he produced a lot of strikeouts, including the 156 he racked up in 1982, a Mets record.

A three-sport star at Prospect High School in Mount Prospect, Illinois, Kingman was a starting center who could already dunk, a rangy wide receiver, and a star pitcher.

He was drafted out of high school by the California Angels and the next year by the Baltimore Orioles, but chose to attend the University of Southern California instead. There, he played for one of the great baseball coaches of all-time in Ron Dedeaux, became an All-American and won the College World Series. In 1970, the San Francisco Giants made Kingman the first pick in the draft.

In 1975, the Mets purchased the contract of "Sky King" for $150,000—a fair price for a player with his power. That year, he hit a career-high 36 homers, setting a new team record. He followed that up with 37 in 1976, earning a spot as the National League's starting right fielder at the All-Star Game for the first time in his career.

On May 13, 1977, Kingman hit one of the longest home runs in the history of Shea Stadium: a 495-foot blast off the Dodgers' Rick Rhoden that sailed over the left-field seats. But a month later, while embroiled in contract squabbles with team owner Don Grant and his batting average hovering just above the Mendoza Line, Kingman was traded to the San Diego Padres for Paul Siebert and Bobby Valentine—part of a flurry of deals known as the "Midnight Massacre" that also saw Tom Seaver shipped to the Cincinnati Reds for a smorgasbord of mediocre players.

A string of injuries and embarrassing confrontations with the press during his time with the Chicago Cubs—he once dumped ice water on reporters at spring training—led to him being traded back to the Mets in February 1981 for Steve Henderson, the de facto "jewel" of the Seaver deal from a few years earlier.

The acerbic New York sports columnist Dick Young, who once wrote that "no man can write cleverly enough to make Dave Kingman appear to be a successful major leaguer," resumed his biting critiques of the towering first baseman/outfielder, who went on to lead the NL in strikeouts that season with 105.

Kingman was on a legendary tear in 1982 before his injury woes returned. He led the NL with 37 homers, but with a batting average of .204, also set a major league mark for the lowest batting average

Dave Kingman is one of only a few major leaguers to play for four teams in one season. In 1977, after being traded by the Mets to the Padres, he was put on waivers and claimed by the Angels. After just 10 games in California, he was traded to the New York Yankees.

for a home run leader. (For a little perspective, Steve Carlton won the Cy Young that year for the Phillies batting .218.) Kingman's franchise-record 156 strikeouts was also tops in the majors, an honor he shared with the Angels' Reggie Jackson.

Kingman's role with the Mets diminished and he was released by the team in January 1984, following another injury-shortened season in which he batted .198 with 13 home runs. He spent his final three years in the majors with the Oakland A's, doing the three things he seemed to do best: hit home runs, strike out, and run afoul of the local media. The low point came when he gift-wrapped a live rat in a pink box and presented it to a female reporter from the *Sacramento Bee* in the press box.

ALL-TIME STRIKEOUT LEADERS
(through 2014)

Rank/Player	Strikeouts
1. Reggie Jackson	2,597
2. Jim Thome	2,548
3. Adam Dunn	2,379
4. Sammy Sosa	2,306
5. Alex Rodriguez*	2,075
6. Andres Galarraga	2,003
7. Jose Canseco	1,942
8. Willie Stargell	1,936
9. Mike Cameron	1,901
10. Mike Schmidt	1,883
11. Fred McGriff	1,882
12. Tony Perez	1,867
13. Bobby Abreu	1,840
14. Derek Jeter	1,840
15. Dave Kingman	1,816

Active

Sidd Finch's

168

MPH Fastball

The April 1, 1985, issue of *Sports Illustrated* introduced the world to a stud pitching prospect in the Mets organization named Sidd Finch (Sidd being short for Siddhartha, title character of the Herman Hesse novel), a Harvard dropout and wannabe Buddhist monk who could throw a baseball 168 miles per hour.

There was just one problem with Finch, one obstacle that stood between him and baseball immortality: he didn't exist. Finch and his incredible story were figments of the imagination of the article's author, the journalist, actor, and amateur sportsman George Plimpton. Plimpton was best known for his sports writing and for co-founding *The Paris Review*, a literary magazine.

According to author Jonathan Dee, who was then an associate editor and Plimpton's personal assistant at *The Paris Review*, Plimpton got the idea to write an April Fools' article profiling an enlightenment-seeking baseball player after reading a spoof piece about a Japanese marathon runner who mistakenly believed that the race lasted 26 days, not 26 miles, and was still out in the wilderness.

"George fell for the story completely," Dee recalled in the 2013 documentary *Plimpton! Starring George Plimpton as Himself*. "It hooked him. He was fooled, he loved *being* fooled in that way and he wanted to do something similar."

Plimpton buried a clue to his true intentions in the *SI* article's sub-heading, which read: "He's a pitcher, part yogi and part recluse. Impressively liberated from our opulent lifestyle, Sidd's deciding about yoga—and his future in baseball." Only the most observant readers caught that the first letters of each of the words spell out "HAPPY APRIL FOOLS DAY—AHFIB." Still, many people—including members of the press—fell for Plimpton's ruse.

The day the story broke, Plimpton was away at a speaking engagement. He'd entrusted Dee, his young assistant, to keep the joke going for as long as possible.

"It was a huge sensation," Dee said. "The phone never stopped ringing all day. The *New York Times* called and said they'd sent a photographer down to the Mets' spring training facility in Florida but couldn't find Sidd there. So I just told them that Sidd is notoriously press-shy."

Sports Illustrated waited two weeks to reveal that the entire episode had been a practical joke, much to the disappointment of Mets fans, who envisioned Finch and his superhuman arm joining a rotation with Doc Gooden, Ron Darling, and Sid Fernandez.

The major league record for the fastest recorded pitch belongs to Cincinnati's Aroldis Chapman. On September 24, 2010, against the Padres, Chapman was clocked at 105.1 MPH. The following season, he was clocked at 106 MPH, but that number is disputed.

"Hitman" Lance Johnson Bags

227

In a dangerous lineup featuring Todd Hundley, Butch Huskey, Jeff Kent, Bernard Gilkey, and Edgardo Alfonzo, Lance Johnson drove this bus. He was the Mets' leadoff hitter, the table setter, the hit man. In 1996, he led the majors with a franchise-record 227 hits.

The 1996 season was Johnson's 10th in the league, most of them spent with the Chicago White Sox. At 32, he was thought to have a lot left in the tank. His legs were still good and he was a threat to steal. One of the better leadoff hitters in the game, he was known for hitting close to .300 with 40 or so steals and double-digits in triples.

The Mets paid almost $3 million to land Johnson as a free agent, and he delivered immediately. Manager Dallas Green was a no-nonsense elder of the game who was supposed to whip the young Mets into shape. The Mets managed an Opening Day win against the St. Louis Cardinals, the team that originally drafted Johnson and eventually traded him to the Chicago White Sox. Johnson got his first Mets hit in a 7–6 win at Shea Stadium. He had an early season eight-game hitting streak. He was remarkably consistent. In the month of April, he had two or more hits in a game 11 times.

Johnson stayed hot through the All-Star break and started the All-Star Game in center field at Veterans Stadium in Philadelphia. It was the only All-Star appearance of his career.

That season he was hitting home runs, triples, and stealing bases. He was a one-man stat sheet. By season's end, Johnson had tallied 227 hits to lead the NL and set a Mets team record while batting .333, the fourth-best average in the National League. His 50 stolen bases was a personal-best and he hit 21 triples to lead the majors, setting another Mets team record.

> *In the month of April, Johnson had two or more hits in a game 11 times.*

By leading the league in triples for a fifth time, Johnson joined the great Stan Musial, Sam Crawford, and Willie Wilson as the only players in major league history to accomplish that feat. He also scored 117 runs, a Mets team record that stood for a few more seasons.

The Mets were well below .500 in 1996, so there was a lot of pressure for them to get over the hump in 1997. Steve Phillips was promoted to GM that July, and he had a mandate to make some changes. With Johnson's production way down from the previous season, the Mets included him in a six-player deal with the Chicago Cubs that brought back outfielder Brian McRae, closer Mel Rojas, and quirky reliever Turk Wendell.

The Mets finished in third place with an 88–74 record. Mets fans liked Johnson but never really got to know him. His one full season as a Met left its mark on the club record book, but the team was able to fill certain needs by moving Johnson out when it did.

Plagued by injuries after leaving the Mets, Johnson never came close to replicating the success he enjoyed in 1996.

John Franco's

276

Saves

John Franco was one of the last of a dying breed: a closer who didn't throw dominating heat. Instead, he nibbled around the outside of the plate with an effective changeup, relied on his control, and occasionally worked in an inside fastball. His tendency to work deep counts soured many a stomach in his 21 major league seasons, 14 spent with his hometown Mets. But he's still a fan-favorite because, more often than not, he got the job done, as evidenced by his club-record 276 saves.

Franco came to New York with minor league outfielder Don Brown in a December 1989 trade with the Cincinnati Reds that cost the Mets the hard-throwing pitcher Kip Gross and the sometimes-wild closer Randy Myers who, with Rob Dibble and Norm Charlton, became part of the "Nasty Boys" bullpen in Cincy that help beat Oakland in the 1990 World Series. In Franco, the Mets felt that they were getting one of the more seasoned closers in the league.

The Brooklyn-born, St. John's–educated lefty was—literally and figuratively—made for New York. He was outspoken and spoke the blue-collar language of the typical baseball fan, so he was immediately accepted. Most importantly, at 28, he still had plenty of life left in his arm.

Franco's detractors would say he was a one-inning-or-less closer and that, unlike contemporaries Mariano Rivera, John Wetteland, or Trevor Hoffman, never reached the 40-save mark in a season. But he did lead the National League in saves on three occasions, including twice with the Mets (33 in 1990 and 30 in 1994). He was also an All-Star four times. His 424 career saves is fourth on the all-time list and most among lefties. He managed to keep his ERA under 3.00 despite playing in 1,245 innings spread out over 1,119 games. Also overlooked is the positive clubhouse influence Franco had on other pitchers. That's a big reason why he was named the Mets' third captain in 2001.

And he never forgot his roots, especially the ones he had with the city's Department of Sanitation. Franco's father, Jim, was a sanitation worker who died on the job of a heart attack in 1987. John honored his father's memory by often wearing an orange Sanitation Department T-shirt under his Mets uniform. Those shirts, which included Franco's name and number 45 on the back, were always a hot seller at Shea.

CAREER LEADERS
Saves

1. Mariano Rivera	652
2. Trevor Hoffman	601
3. Lee Smith	478
4. John Franco	424
5. Billy Wagner	422

CAREER LEADERS
Blown Saves

1. Goose Gossage	112
2. Rollie Fingers	109
3. Jeff Reardon	106
4. Lee Smith	103
5. John Franco	101
5. Bruce Sutter	101

Mike Piazza and John Franco are in the middle of things as the Mets celebrate after defeating the St. Louis Cardinals in Game 5 of the 2000 NLCS. *(Mike Albans)*

JOHN FRANCO AND THE PETE ROSE SCANDAL

During his time in Cincinnati, John Franco was front and center for one of the most controversial episodes in the history of the game: the investigation into whether Reds manager Pete Rose ever bet on baseball. Franco was one of nine people (but the only player) named in an MLB-sanctioned report to have had direct knowledge of Rose's gambling. He admitted to checking football scores for Rose in the players' lounge during games but claimed he didn't know if Rose bet on baseball. In 1989, Rose accepted a lifetime ban from the sport but denied any wrongdoing for 15 years.

On May 11, 1996—John Franco Day at Shea Stadium to celebrate his 300th career save—the guest of honor never threw a pitch but he did throw some punches after tearing out of the bullpen to take part in a fifth-inning brawl against the Chicago Cubs. That was John. He stuck up for his teammates.

Three years later, at age 38, Franco made his first trip to the postseason as the Mets beat the Diamondbacks in the NLDS before falling to Atlanta in the NLCS. In 2000, he played in his first World Series and was perfect in just over three innings of work. He was even credited with the Mets' sole win of the series.

September 17, 2001, was another memorable day in Franco's career: the day of the first Mets game following the terrorist attacks of 9/11. In Pittsburgh, the Mets badly wanted to win to help begin the process of healing for an anguished fan base watching back home. A three-run ninth put the Mets ahead 4–1. Fittingly, it was Franco, the team's only native New Yorker, who got the win.

In time, Franco lost the closer's job to Armando Benitez and he missed the entire 2002 season due to injury. Following a disappointing 2004 season in which he went 2–7 with a 5.28 ERA, the 44-year-old became a free agent. He agreed to a one-year deal with the Astros, with whom he spent his final season.

Since retiring, Franco has continued to make special appearances on behalf of the Mets and is a familiar face around spring training. On March 29, 2009, he threw out the very first ceremonial pitch in the history of Citi Field to open a Big East game between his alma mater, St. John's, and Georgetown.

Piazza Becomes Home Run King Among Catchers with No.

352

Mike Piazza is arguably the greatest hitting catcher of all time—if not the greatest, then certainly in the conversation with Carlton Fisk, Yogi Berra, and Johnny Bench. On May 5, 2004, in front of a raucous Shea Stadium crowd, Piazza made baseball history by becoming the all-time home run leader among catchers when he drove a 3–1 pitch from San Francisco's Jerome Williams off the bottom of the scoreboard in right-center.

Piazza's 352nd homer as a catcher—and 363rd of his career—moved him past Fisk, a Hall of Famer and 11-time All-Star who split his 24-year career between the Boston Red Sox and Chicago White Sox.

Originally drafted by the Dodgers, Piazza was selected as a favor to then-manager Tommy Lasorda, who was close friends with Piazza's father, and godfather to the catcher's brother. He went on to win the 1993 NL Rookie of the Year with 35 home runs and 112 RBI while batting .318.

On May 14, 1998, Piazza was traded by Los Angeles to the Florida Marlins. Just eight days later, Mets fans' hearts skipped a beat when they heard on WFAN's *Mike and the Mad Dog* program that the best-hitting catcher in the game was now headed to Queens. Who the Mets were giving up in the deal with Florida was almost inconsequential (though, for the record, it was pitchers Geoff Goetz and Ed Yarnall and outfielder Preston Wilson). Mets general manager Steve Phillips was, temporarily, a hero.

Fans immediately welcomed Piazza to New York. The slugger heard his share of boos during an early slump, and his struggles

MIKE PIAZZA'S 427 CAREER HOME RUNS BY POSITION

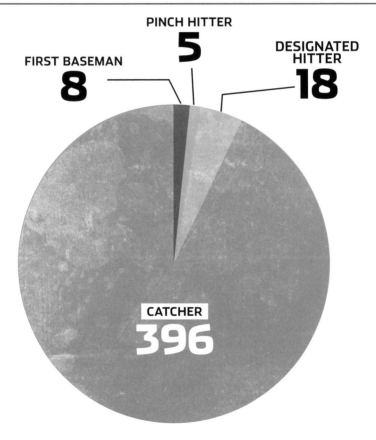

PINCH HITTER
5

DESIGNATED HITTER
18

FIRST BASEMAN
8

CATCHER
396

at the plate became talk-radio fodder. But Mike eventually caught fire and gave fans hope for the future by hitting 23 homers in just 394 at-bats. He also had an amazing 76 RBI in just 109 games. The team finished in second place with an impressive 88–74 record.

In 1999, Piazza had his best offensive season as a Met, batting .303 and tying a career-high with 40 home runs. He also drove in 124 runs.

Piazza's rivalry with Yankees pitcher Roger Clemens boiled over during the 2000 season when Piazza was beaned by Clemens during a regular season game and suffered a concussion. When the teams met again that October in the World Series, a clearly off-his-rocker Clemens grabbed a shard of Piazza's shattered bat and chucked it in the catcher's direction as he was running toward first.

He called a decent game but defensively, Piazza's play left much to be desired. He led the league in stolen bases allowed on 10 occasions and errors as a catcher four times. One lived with those shortcomings because of what he was able to do with his bat, like on that emotional night 10 days after 9/11.

The Mets hosted the Atlanta Braves. The Shea scoreboard had an outline of the Twin Towers on it and on that night they turned off the lights on them and placed a ribbon over the buildings. There was a lengthy pre-game tribute to the victims. Piazza was visibly moved by the proceedings, as was anyone with an ounce of humanity who happened to be watching at home or in the stands.

People needed a return to normalcy. Families of some of the victims were at this game and in the eighth inning, something magical happened. The Mets were trailing 2–1 with one man on when Piazza came to the plate. Fans hoped he might go deep, then he answered their appeal by driving a Steve Karsay pitch deep into the batter's eye behind center field. Fans went berserk. As Piazza rounded the bases, someone in the crowd held up a sign that read "We Believe." Others waved little American flags. All of

MIKE PIAZZA'S 427 CAREER HOME RUNS —
LEFTIES VS. RIGHTIES

⚾ = VS. RIGHTIES   ⚾ = VS. LEFTIES

104 HOME RUNS

323 HOME RUNS

Mike's teammates were waiting to mob him at home plate. The Mets won the game 3–2. Afterward, the Braves had to admit that, under those unique circumstances, they were "okay" taking the loss.

On May 5, 2004, Piazza set a major league mark for most home runs by a catcher with his 352nd homer. It would have happened earlier but they didn't count some of his home runs as a designated hitter in interleague contests. With his long looping swing, and top-heavy bat, the Mets catcher jacked one out that hit a famous Jackie Robinson quote attached to the scoreboard in right field. Fans and teammates stood and clapped. It was the second-most-famous home run he'd hit to date.

Piazza also had an amazing 76 RBI in 109 games

Later that season, the Mets held a day in Piazza's honor, inviting Hall of Fame catchers Berra, Bench, Fisk, and Mets legend Gary Carter to participate.

Because Piazza played during baseball's Steroid Era, there was suspicion on the part of some Hall of Fame voters—but no concrete evidence—that his gaudy stats got a boost from performance-enhancing drugs. He was passed over for election to the Hall again in 2015, his third year of eligibility.

Tommie Agee's

480

Foot Blast

In its 45 seasons as the home of Mets baseball, Shea Stadium never had anyone hit a ball into the upper deck in fair territory... except once. On April 10, 1969, New York's Tommie Agee made history against the Montreal Expos.

Larry Jaster was on the mound for Montreal that day—the same Larry Jaster who, a year earlier with the Cardinals, took a no-hitter into the seventh inning against the Mets before giving up a single to catcher Greg Goossen. But Agee had Jaster figured out. He was 5-for-8 with four career homers against the tall lefty. With two outs in the bottom of the second inning, Jaster dealt Agee a fastball low and inside. Agee connected with it perfectly, hitting a line drive to left that landed in a sea of empty green seats about 480 feet from home plate.

It's too bad that not many people witnessed it. There were only about 8,600 fans in the park that afternoon and the game wasn't televised.

Agee sent another ball out of the park off Jaster in the bottom of the seventh en route to a 4–2 New York win.

A big, strong center fielder, Agee was a great all-around athlete as a kid and a four-sport star in high school, playing football, basketball, and baseball as well as running track. On the baseball diamond, he batted .390 and also pitched, helping earn him a scholarship to play ball for Grambling State University. In his first game for the Tigers, he hit a home run over the left-field fence, another one over the center-field fence, and a third one over the right-field fence. Then he hit the ball so far into center that he got an inside-the-park home run.

Agee was once told by a Giants scout that he'd never make it to the majors. But after just one year at Grambling, he was fielding offers from teams left and right. He'd end up a bonus baby with the Cleveland Indians but was later dealt to the Chicago White Sox. In 1966, his first full season in the majors, he was named the American League Rookie of the Year. With 44 steals that year to go along with 22 homers and 86 RBI, Agee reminded some of a young Willie Mays.

In December 1967, the two-time All-Star was traded to the Mets with utility player Al Weis for slugger Tommy Davis, catcher Buddy Booker, and pitchers Jack Fisher (who had a league-leading 24 losses in 1965) and Billy Wynne.

The Mets were well represented in National League MVP voting in 1969, with three players finishing among the top eight vote-getters:

	Team	Vote points
1. Willie McCovey	Giants	265
2. Tom Seaver	Mets	243
3. Hank Aaron	Braves	188
4. Pete Rose	Reds	127
5. Ron Santo	Cubs	124
6. Tommie Agee	Mets	89
8. Cleon Jones	Mets	82

Mets general manager Johnny Murphy snookered the White Sox but it took a little while for the Mets and their fans to feel the impact of the deal. Agee was beaned by Cardinals ace Bob Gibson on the very first pitch the Mets faced in spring training in 1968. Back then, there were no concussion protocols. Players played through injuries because it was their job. He went 0-for-34 at one point that season (tying the Mets' record for batting futility set by Don Zimmer in 1962) and hit only .217.

Agee rebounded strongly the following season, batting .271 with a career-high 26 home runs and 76 RBI. He was also among the Mets' leading hitters in the NLCS, batting .357 with two home runs and four RBI in New York's three-game sweep of the Atlanta Braves.

RECORD ROUND-TRIPPERS: THE LONGEST HOME RUNS IN SHEA STADIUM HISTORY

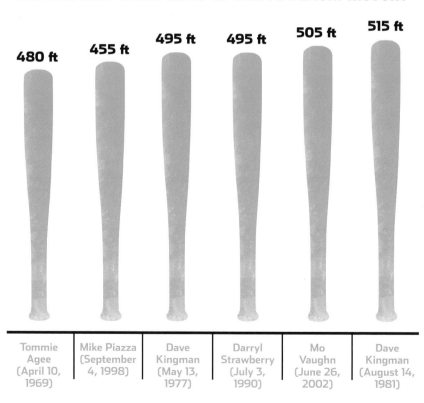

480 ft	455 ft	495 ft	495 ft	505 ft	515 ft
Tommie Agee (April 10, 1969)	Mike Piazza (September 4, 1998)	Dave Kingman (May 13, 1977)	Darryl Strawberry (July 3, 1990)	Mo Vaughn (June 26, 2002)	Dave Kingman (August 14, 1981)

As valuable as Agee was with his bat, he really solidified his place in Mets history with his glove. He and his childhood friend, Cleon Jones, formed two-thirds of one of the best outfields the Mets have ever had. In Game 3 of the 1969 World Series, with the Mets and the Baltimore Orioles tied at one game apiece, Agee led off with a home run in the bottom of the first inning, then made two spectacular catches that saved as many as five runs.

Baltimore trailed 3–0 in the fourth but had runners on first and third with two out when Orioles catcher Elrod Hendricks hit a long, high drive to deep left-center. Agee sprinted across the grass toward Jones, reached out and grabbed the ball backhanded in the webbing of his glove and held onto it while he bounced off the wall at the 396-foot marker. As the Shea Stadium crowd roared, he jogged back to the dugout with the ball still poking out of his glove.

Then, with the Mets ahead 4–0 in the seventh, the Orioles loaded the bases with two outs. Baltimore center fielder Paul Blair got a hit to deep right-center. Agee ran to his left and made a diving, skidding one-handed grab just as the ball was about to land on the warning track. Blair was robbed of a possible game-tying, inside-the-park home run. The Mets went on to win that game, the next two, and their first World Series trophy.

Agee gave the Mets five of his prime years in the game. Traded to the Houston Astros in November 1972, he split his final season between the Astros and Cardinals before retiring in 1973 at the relatively young age of 30. His knees were shot.

No one who watched him play would ever forget the excitement he brought to Shea Stadium. But, just to make sure, the team painted his name, uniform number (20), and the date of his mammoth 480-foot home run on the wall up in Section 48 where the ball hit.

Agee died of a heart attack in 2001 at the age of 58. A charitable organization, the Tommie Agee Foundation, was established in his memory and raises funds for a number of national and local charities including Ronald McDonald House, the Heart Association, Make-A-Wish Foundation, and Habitat for Humanity.

Jose Reyes: Mets Record

696

At-Bats

Good leadoff hitters are hard to find. Typically, the best ones can get a base hit, steal second, then get knocked in by the No. 2, No. 3, or No. 4 hitter. Jose Reyes was that guy. His on-base percentage was never great but when he got up, he created excitement. That's why he had 696 at-bats in 2005, setting a Mets franchise record that may never be broken.

Reyes, a skinny kid from the Dominican Republic who used his signing bonus to buy a mini mart for his father to run, was arguably the greatest free-agent signing the Mets have ever made. He rose through the prospect ranks quickly to earn Player of the Year honors in Class A. The Mets were so sure that Reyes was their shortstop of the future that in 2002, they traded incumbent Rey Ordonez to the Tampa Bay Rays. An injury to veteran Rey Sanchez led to Reyes being summoned from AAA Norfolk.

Just shy of 20, Jose went 2-for-4 with two runs scored in his major league debut on June 10, 2003. He became a full-time player in that first season before an ankle injury shut him down.

In 2004, the Mets signed Japanese import Kaz Matsui to play shortstop and moved Reyes to second. The shift seemed to agree with Jose. He was hitting over .300 and still being heralded as the future of the franchise. But then came a series of hamstring injuries that thrust the organization into panic mode. Some in the Mets clubhouse snickered at Reyes' apparent lack of durability and questioned his heart.

DID YOU KNOW?

Phillies leadoff hitter Jimmy Rollins holds the all-time single-season record with 716 at-bats, set in 2007.

Jose went through four rehab assignments, worked with three different fitness experts, and even tried a new way of running to reduce the chances of reinjuring himself. But after he got through a season of winter-league ball in the Dominican unscathed, he ditched the specialists and went back to good old-fashioned stretching.

Fans who wondered if they'd ever see the "real" Jose Reyes didn't have long to wait. Looking reinvigorated, the 22-year-old led the NL in triples (17) and steals (60) in 2005. His club record 696 at-bats was an indication of how valuable he'd become to the Mets. Apart from the occasional fielding snafu, he was meeting or exceeding expectations in virtually every way.

And he was quick. *Really* quick. Jose insisted there were faster people back in the Dominican, but it's likely they were sprinters, not baseball players. David Wright marveled at Reyes' speed.

"Everybody knows he's fast," Wright said. "As a base runner, he definitely has to be one of the fastest. The turns that he makes, he cuts corners, the way that he accelerates, it's amazing."

Jose's value to the Mets continued to climb in the years that followed. More hits, more triples, more home runs...even a league-leading 78 steals in 2007, still a single-season club record. In 2008, he passed Mookie Wilson as the Mets' all-time stolen base leader when he got No. 282 in September against the Nationals. He also had his first 200-hit season—the first Met since Lance Johnson reached 200 in 1996.

David Wright and Jose Reyes congratulate each other after a 2006 victory over the Braves. *(Scott Cunningham)*

Mets skipper Willie Randolph appreciated Reyes' importance to the team. Like Reyes, Randolph had once been a stud baseball prospect thrust under the microscope in the world's biggest media market. Here was someone who could play the aggressive style Randolph loved, "Willieball," which is probably why he tolerated his shortstop's celebratory antics on the field and in the dugout. His critiques of Reyes tended to be more measured and delivered in private. Randolph's replacement, Jerry Manuel, showed less restraint.

"I think the best baseball is ahead of Jose Reyes," Manuel told MLB.com. "I think Jose Reyes is a stallion. He's out of control at times, but that's due to anxiety, not [a lack of] intelligence. All he needs is responsibility for the maturation process. He wants to be the best."

OF 269 TOTAL BASES IN 2005...

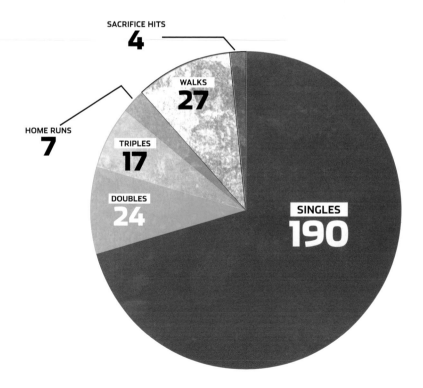

After another injury-shortened 2009 season in which he appeared in only 36 games, Reyes responded with back-to-back All-Star seasons.

The "Reyes watch" was on. Would he stay? Would he go? Mets GM Sandy Alderson wasn't prepared to break the bank for Reyes, especially after team owner Fred Wilpon went on record as saying he didn't believe Reyes deserved a superstar's contract.

On September 28, 2011, the last day of the season, Reyes heard 15,000 fans chant "JOSE! JOSE! JOSE!" It's something he'd experienced many times before, but this was different. This time, Mets fans were letting him know how much they hoped this would not be his last game as a Met. They cheered loudly for him when he led off the game with a bunt single to third off the Reds' Edinson Volquez. Then the game took a peculiar turn. Reyes walked back to the dugout, racked his bat and helmet, and took his seat on the bench.

Unbeknownst to the crowd, Reyes—in the lead for the National League batting crown with a .337 average—had asked manager Terry Collins to pull him if he got a hit in his first at-bat. Collins, in his first year on the job and wanting to build trust with his players, reluctantly honored the shortstop's request.

That Reyes was about to become the first Met ever to win a batting title didn't matter to fans who paid good money to watch him play. Cheers quickly turned to boos.

That off-season, the Mets had an exclusive negotiating period with Reyes, though it was never clear if the team ever made him an offer. Ultimately, he received the megadeal he'd been seeking: a six-year, $106 million contract from the Marlins.

Omar Minaya Flies

2,800

Miles to Fire
Willie Randolph

Baseball managers know they're hired to get fired. Very few walk away on their own terms, and Willie Randolph understood that well. But the Mets skipper did not expect his boss, general manager Omar Minaya, to hop on a plane and fly 2,800 miles to Anaheim, California, to fire him in the middle of the night.

Minaya hired Randolph…and had the chance to fire him after the 2007 Mets lost 12 of their last 17 games and missed the playoffs. The Wilpons left Willie's fate in Omar's hands. And Omar wanted to bring him back.

A year later, the Mets were a big-budget squad expected to not only play meaningful games in September, but compete for a World Series title in October. Even with a roster featuring stars Carlos Beltran, Carlos Delgado, Jose Reyes, Johan Santana, and David Wright, the team was below .500—no doubt still haunted by the previous season's collapse. Speculation about Randolph's job status was growing daily while the chants of "Fire Willie!" were getting louder at Shea Stadium and on New York's sports-talk-radio stations.

Randolph wasn't oblivious to the chatter. He'd heard it. Everyone had. The tension became a distraction, and the last thing the Mets needed was another distraction. A five-game losing streak in early June really kicked the "Willie Watch" into overdrive.

Tired of wondering when or if the ax would fall, Randolph asked Minaya to fire him before the team left for a six-game Western road trip if that's what he was planning. "I actually asked him," Randolph recalled for the *New York Times*. "I said, 'Omar, do this now. If you're going to do this, do this now. I know you've got a lot of pressure on you, but if I'm not the guy to lead this team, then don't let me get on this plane.' I did say that to him."

So when Minaya let Randolph fly to California, it appeared his job was safe for the time being. It was not. The very next day, Minaya made up his mind that he needed to fire his manager. And he felt the right way to do it was face-to-face. So he caught a flight to Anaheim, went to the team hotel, and waited to deliver the news in person. When Willie returned to the hotel following that night's game, a 9–6 win over the Angels, he learned that he was no longer manager of the Mets.

Joining Randolph in the "Midnight Massacre" were pitching coach Rick Peterson and first-base coach Tom Nieto.

The move was announced in an email from the team at 12:14 AM West Coast time, making it 3:14 AM back in New York.

Bench coach Jerry Manuel, who'd won AL Manager of the Year in 2000 when he was with the Chicago White Sox, was named interim manager. Under Manuel, the Mets won 55 of their final 93 games to finish second in the division with a respectable 89–73 record. They very nearly made the playoffs, but were eliminated from postseason play on the last day of the regular season by the Florida Marlins for the second straight year.

In four seasons as Mets manager, Randolph compiled a 302–253 record and his .544 winning percentage was second on the club's all-time list. In 2006, he guided the team to a 97–65 record as the Mets won their first division title in 18 years but lost Game 7 of the NLCS to the eventual World Series–champion St. Louis Cardinals.

Maybe Randolph, who took a lot of heat for not getting the most out of his star players, wasn't the right man to lead the Mets. Or maybe he did the best he could with a group that was showing its age at key positions. That's open to debate. But the timing and manner with which he was let go drew widespread condemnation from fans and media and did nothing to alter the perception of the Mets as an organization prone to bungling front-office moves.

Daily News columnist Bill Madden called Randolph's firing "shameful, indecent, undignified."

Willie, a dignified baseball man if ever there was one, deserved better.

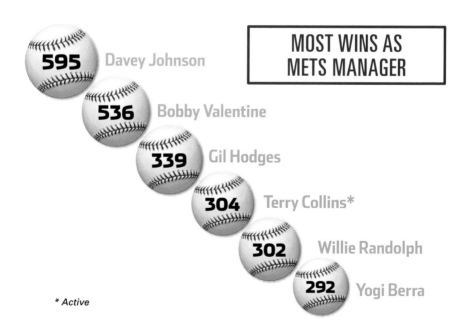

MOST WINS AS METS MANAGER

595 Davey Johnson

536 Bobby Valentine

339 Gil Hodges

304 Terry Collins*

302 Willie Randolph

292 Yogi Berra

* Active

Roberto Clemente, Jon Matlack, and hit No.

3,000

In New York, Jon Matlack combined with Tom Seaver and Jerry Koosman to form one of the best starting rotations in baseball. In Pittsburgh—and, it turns out, much of the Latino baseball universe—he's the answer to a trivia question: Who surrendered Roberto Clemente's 3,000th and final career hit?

The date was September 30, 1972. Clemente, the Pirates' 38-year-old Puerto Rican superstar, smacked a long double to left-center field off the rookie Matlack in the fourth inning to become the 11th man in major league history to reach the 3,000-hit plateau. Clemente's double sparked a three-run Pirate rally that resulted in a 5–0 victory over the Mets.

Clemente said later that the ball he hit was a curveball. "It was the same pitch [Matlack] struck me out on in the first inning," Roberto said.

Clemente played one more inning in the field and then, as he returned to the dugout, Mets veteran Willie Mays trotted over from the visitors' dugout and offered his congratulations while the photographers and TV cameras took pictures. At the time, Mays and Hank Aaron were the only active players with 3,000 or more hits.

Mets shortstop Jim Fregosi retrieved the ball, but Matlack didn't realize the importance of what had just happened until the second-base umpire, Doug Harvey, presented it to Clemente.

"I was a 22-year-old rookie that had absolutely no clue this baseball icon was sitting on 2,999 when I went out to pitch that game," Matlack recalled in a 2011 interview with the *New York Times*.

Clemente's 3,000th hit would be his last. Three months later, on December 31, he died in a plane crash off the coast of Puerto Rico while delivering relief supplies to earthquake victims in Nicaragua.

As Clemente's legend grew, and the tale of his last game was told and retold, an entire generation of Latin American prospects became familiar with the name "Jon Matlack," if only because of his Clemente connection.

Matlack made the Mets out of spring training in 1972 and got off to a 6–0 start with a 1.95 ERA in the first two months of the season. He finished with a 15–10 record and career-best 2.32 ERA to win National League Rookie of the Year honors.

The tall and gangly pitcher who bore more than a passing resemblance to actor Fred Gwynne (aka Herman Munster) was far better than his 82–81 career Mets record would suggest. In 1974, for example, he went 13–15 but had a 2.41 ERA, pitched 14 complete games, and led the majors with seven shutouts. Imagine what Matlack might have accomplished with a little more run support.

Along with a distinctive delivery that culminated with a high leg kick, durability was Matlack's calling card. On May 8, 1973, he was struck in the head by a nasty line drive off the bat of Atlanta's Marty Perez. He suffered a hairline fracture of his skull but was back on the mound just 11 days later to pitch six shutout innings at Pittsburgh. He ended up winning 14 games that season as the Mets won their second division title.

CAREER RUN SUPPORT FOR JON MATLACK (AS STARTER)
Out of 318 career starts...

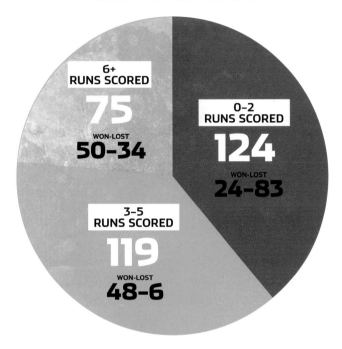

6+
RUNS SCORED
75
WON-LOST
50–34

0–2
RUNS SCORED
124
WON-LOST
24–83

3–5
RUNS SCORED
119
WON-LOST
48–6

Maybe his best outing came in Game 2 of the 1973 NLCS against Cincinnati. That day, Matlack held the vaunted "Big Red Machine" of Pete Rose, Johnny Bench, and Joe Morgan to just two hits, both courtesy of Andy Kosco.

Matlack was equally impressive in the World Series, giving up just three hits in six innings in Game 1. However, Oakland scored two runs on a Felix Millan error in the third, and held on for the 2–1 victory. Matlack won Game 4, surrendering just one run in eight innings, and was sent to the mound again for the decisive seventh game. In the third inning, he gave up a pair of two-run homers to Bert Campaneris and Reggie Jackson—the only two home runs Oakland would hit the entire series—and the A's went on to defeat the Mets, 5–2.

Matlack was an All-Star for the Mets for the next three seasons, sharing MVP honors in the 1975 game with the Cubs' Bill "Mad Dog" Madlock.

4,800

Pounds. That's a Big Apple.

The Yankees are known for their stodgy, corporate image. They have a hard time letting their hair down. Literally. This is the ballclub that still hasn't lifted its ridiculous ban on long hair and facial growth beyond the well-trimmed mustache. The Mets, conversely, have tended to not take themselves quite so seriously.

One wonders if the marketing campaign the team launched in May 1980, the one with the slogan "The Magic is Back," was another way to distance itself from Baseball, Inc. As part of this campaign, the Mets built a giant Home Run Apple out of fiberboard that would rise out of an equally enormous, upside-down magician's top hat behind the center-field wall whenever the team would hit a home run.

Originally emblazoned with the slogan "Mets Magic" in cursive writing, it was changed a few years later to read "Home Run" in big block letters.

Early reviews of the apple—and the slogan—were decidedly mixed. Fans just weren't feeling the magic. Ed Kranepool, Jon Matlack, Tom Seaver, and other '70s fan favorites were gone and Darryl Strawberry and Dwight Gooden were still years away. The 1980 Mets under manager Joe Torre finished fifth in their division at 67–95. As a *team*, they hit only 61 home runs, the same amount Yankee slugger Roger Maris hit by himself in 1961.

Fans pose in front of the Shea Stadium Home Run Apple, which now resides at Citi Field. *(Tim Clayton)*

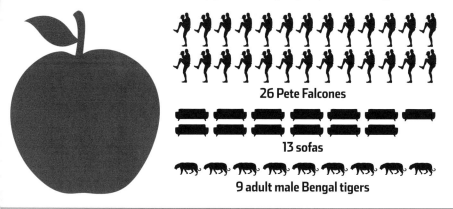

The Citi Field Home Run Apple is roughly equal in weight to:

26 Pete Falcones

13 sofas

9 adult male Bengal tigers

In hindsight, a more accurate slogan might have been, "Hang On, the Magic Will Be Back Soon."

Management could be forgiven for trying to put a positive marketing spin on the franchise, but the apple became a Mets icon—something for the kids to get excited about. Something *fun*. And, when all is said and done, that's what the game should be all about.

When Citi Field opened in 2009, fans wondered what the team would do with the Home Run Apple. Ultimately, the Mets decided to bring the tradition with them to Citi Field, but they built a new, shinier apple nearly four times bigger than the previous one. Located in the center-field stands, it weighs about 4,800 pounds… but closer to 8,500 pounds when one factors in all the hydraulics and other equipment underneath. By comparison, the old apple weighed only 582 pounds.

The original apple wasn't thrown away like last week's produce. Instead, it was placed inside the bullpen gate, then moved to outside of the stadium at the entrance to the Jackie Robinson Rotunda.

Bobby V. Fined

$5,000

for Dugout Disguise

Over the course of seven seasons, Bobby Valentine managed 1,003 games for the Mets, winning 536. Only Davey Johnson (595) won more. Valentine also guided the club to its first World Series appearance in 14 years. But his most memorable game as Mets skipper occurred on June 9, 1999, an interleague tilt with the visiting Toronto Blue Jays. That night, Bobby's unprecedented defiance of an umpire's call would lighten his wallet by $5,000.

The Mets and Jays were tied 3–3 in the top of the 12th inning. With one out and a runner on first, home-plate umpire Randy Marsh awarded Toronto infielder Craig Grebeck first base due to a catcher's interference call on Mike Piazza. It was an unusual call—unusual enough for Valentine to come out of the dugout to dispute it. Words were exchanged and Valentine got tossed.

Under virtually any other circumstances, the story would have ended there because managers get ejected all the time…and they *stay* ejected. There's actually a rule stating that ejected personnel have to remain in the clubhouse until the game is over or change into street clothes and either leave the park or take a seat in the stands.

Valentine went to the clubhouse and put on a pair of dark sunglasses to hide his eyes, a cap to help conceal his face, and a fake mustache made from eye-black stickers. Then he snuck back into the dugout. Not just to watch, but to *manage*. With runners on first and second and no outs in the bottom of the 14th inning, he ordered a sacrifice bunt that successfully advanced the runners. A few minutes later, a Rey Ordonez single brought home the winning run.

The umpire crew never spotted Valentine in the dugout, but TV cameras did. The next day, images of the manager in his hysterical getup spread like wildfire through the media. He claimed the stunt was an attempt at humor—mission accomplished!—but the league was not amused. National League president Len Coleman slapped Valentine with a two-game suspension and a $5,000 fine.

New York's 4–3 win over Toronto kicked off an 18–5 run for the Mets, who ended the year tied with Cincinnati for the wild-card. They beat the Reds in a one-game playoff and the Diamondbacks in the NLDS before falling to Atlanta in the NLCS.

A utility man during his playing days, which included a two-year stint (1977–78) with the Mets, Valentine was a hard-working manager who stressed the fundamentals: defense and base running. At times, he was upbeat to the point of being hyper. With the famously tough New York press, the Connecticut native had the ability to speak fluently, coherently, and at length about the game. He talked so often that it had the positive effect of taking some pressure off his players.

 **DID YOU KNOW?**

A 2002 recipient of the Branch Rickey Award for outstanding community service, Bobby Valentine was one of the first local celebrities to visit with workers at Ground Zero after 9/11. Unfortunately, he's remembered more for ill-timed and inaccurate comments he made on the 12-year anniversary of the terrorist attacks in which he accused the Yankees of being "AWOL" in the weeks immediately following 9/11. That gaffe cost Valentine a job as an analyst on TBS.

On the flipside, some found his brutal honesty and inflated ego to be off-putting...especially the veterans. He was guilty of sometimes overthinking the game with double switches and defensive replacements.

Valentine also had a sometimes rocky relationship with general manager Steve Phillips, especially after Phillips fired three of Valentine's coaches—pitching coach Bob Apodaca, hitting coach Tom Robson, and bullpen coach Randy Niemann—and picked their replacements himself. It was a controversial move that certainly looked like an attempt to get Valentine to quit. He didn't, but was fired three years later after the Mets finished last in the NL East despite having one of the highest payrolls in baseball.

DID THE FINE FIT THE CRIME?

$500,000: The sum Red Sox owner John Henry was fined in 2009 for publicly slamming the sport's revenue-sharing rules.

$225,000: Yankees owner George Steinbrenner shelled out this amount in 1990 for tampering with the Dave Winfield trade.

$135,000: The fine paid by Mets star Keith Hernandez in 1986 as punishment for illegal drug use. This figure represented 10 percent of his annual salary.

$50,000: Yankees hurler Roger Clemens was $50,000 poorer after throwing the jagged barrel of a shattered bat toward Mets catcher Mike Piazza in Game 2 of the 2000 World Series.

$25,000: The penalty levied against Reds owner Marge Schott in 1995 for racist comments about blacks and Jews. Schott was also suspended from baseball for one year.

$10,000: The price Reds manager Pete Rose paid in 1988 for pushing umpire David Pallone. Rose was also suspended for 20 days.

$1,000: The fine paid by Giants closer Brian Wilson for wearing Day-Glo orange cleats in a 2010 game against the Marlins.

$200: Rangers manager Ron Washington was fined this modest sum in 2012 for his role in an altercation during a spring training game. He responded by shipping a box of 20,000 pennies to MLB headquarters in New York.

8,019

Games Without a No-Hitter

It was a streak that lasted 51 seasons and 8,019 regular season games. But finally, on June 1, 2012, Johan Santana pitched the first no-hitter in the history of the Mets, an 8–0 win over the visiting St. Louis Cardinals.

Quite a few other Met pitchers came close, though none quite as close or as often as Tom Seaver. On July 9, 1969, Seaver retired the first 25 batters in a victory over the Cubs before Jim Qualls, the last guy off the bench, singled with one out in the ninth. We'd barely gotten over that one when, three years later, Seaver got to one out in the ninth against the Padres before Leron Lee singled up the middle. Then, on September 4, 1975, Seaver got two out in the ninth before Joe Wallis of the Cubs lined a single to right field. Tom did eventually get his no-hitter, but as a member of the Cincinnati Reds.

Gary Gentry, David Cone, and Tom Glavine each made it to the eighth inning before their no-hit bids were spoiled. In all, Mets pitchers amassed 38 one-hitters before Santana broke the curse.

Over the years, superstitious Mets fans had become so accustomed to the near-misses that they created their own lingo to alert friends that if they weren't watching a particular game, they should tune in...just in case. One dared not utter the words "no-hitter" in case the baseball gods were eavesdropping.

Going into that game against the Cardinals, Santana was being closely monitored for signs of fatigue. He had missed all of 2011 recovering from left-shoulder surgery and manager Terry Collins wanted to limit the big lefty to a strict 115-pitch count.

Santana reached that mark earlier than expected but informed his manager he wasn't coming out of the game. There was a tense moment in the top of the sixth inning when ex-Met Carlos Beltran, in his first return appearance at Citi Field, drilled a line drive down the third-base line, but umpire Adrian Johnson signaled foul ball. Replays from multiple angles suggested the ball should have been ruled a double, but the umpire's call stood.

And then, in the seventh, Mike Baxter stumbled shoulder-first into the wall to make a beautiful catch on Yadier Molina's line-drive to left. Baxter left the game clutching his left forearm.

At the end of each inning, Mets fans stood and cheered a little louder for Santana, the two-time Cy Young Award winner and four-time All-Star inching toward that elusive no-no.

Santana threw 134 pitches, striking out eight and walking five. He fanned David Freese to secure the final out and his place in Mets lore, sending the crowd into a frenzy. Teammates rushed from every direction—the outfield, the dugout, the bullpen—to mob Johan while the scoreboard flashed "No-Han."

The Mets had high hopes for Santana when they acquired him from the Minnesota Twins in January 2008 for young outfielder

As of 2014, the only major league team without a no-hitter was the San Diego Padres, a streak encompassing the club's entire 45-year existence.

PITCHERS WITH MOST NO-HITTERS BROKEN UP IN SEVENTH INNING OR LATER

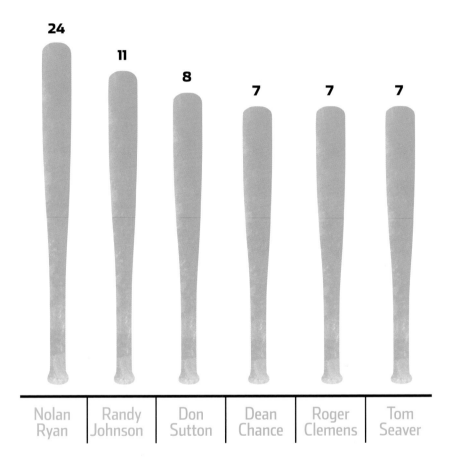

Nolan Ryan	Randy Johnson	Don Sutton	Dean Chance	Roger Clemens	Tom Seaver
24	11	8	7	7	7

Carlos Gomez plus pitching prospects Philip Humber, Kevin Mulvey, and Deolis Guerra. They opened the vault for the 29-year-old Venezuelan, inking him to a six-year, $137.5 million contract extension—the richest ever for a pitcher—with the expectation that he would be the ace to lead them back to the postseason.

He certainly looked the part in the early going. In his first Mets season, he went 16–7 with a league-leading 2.53 ERA and finished third in voting for the Cy Young. But the team was eliminated from postseason play on the last day of the regular season by the Marlins. The Mets never placed higher than fourth in the NL East for the remainder of Santana's time in New York.

Another shoulder injury sidelined Johan for the entire 2013 season. Sensing Santana was no longer the star pitcher he once had been, the Mets paid him a $5.5 million buyout to avoid being responsible for his $25 million option for the following season.

Santana threw 134 pitches, striking out eight and walking five.

Although there was some talk Santana might return to the Mets at a reduced rate, he instead signed a free agent minor league deal with the Baltimore Orioles. But he tore an Achilles' tendon during an extended spring training start and never played in 2014. Mounting injuries and a diminishing fastball clocked in the low 80s cast doubt on Santana's future in the major leagues.

Have the Mets been guilty of doling out some terrible contracts in pursuit of respectability? Yes. Did they want a better return on their mammoth investment in Santana than a 46–34 (.575) regular season record and zero playoff games? Sure. But Santana was a true competitor who gave his all every time he took the hill. Hopefully, he'll be remembered as much for that as for that one night in June when he was unhittable.

56,188

See First Mets-Yankees Interleague Game

On June 16, 1997, 56,188 people packed Yankee Stadium to witness the first-ever regular season game between the Mets and Yankees. The teams had already met over 100 times in exhibition, many of those games part of the Mayor's Trophy series. But it wasn't enough to satiate fans' bloodlust. Before interleague play, the rivalry was like an itch that could never be scratched.

The concept of interleague play had existed for a long time, and was considered by the league as far back as 1958. It finally came into existence in 1997 to help counter the effects of the 1994 MLB strike that had decimated interest in baseball, and make way for more teams in the playoffs The league expanded to 30 teams the following year.

Not all interleague matchups were created equal, of course. Interleague play would introduce variety in the schedule but was also designed to ignite local rivalries, so Twins vs. Rockies was never going to be as sexy as, say, Cubs vs. White Sox, A's vs.

Giants, or Mets vs. Yankees. Those were the marquee matchups commissioner Bud Selig and company dreamt about.

Fans too young to remember the hate-fueled pennant races between the Giants and Dodgers and both teams' frequent postseason battles with the Yankees got a taste of that atmosphere in the days leading up to the three-game "Subway Series" in the Bronx.

With bragging rights for New York City at stake, nobody wanted to win the series more than Yankees owner George Steinbrenner, who always hated being upstaged by the Mets, on the field or in the press. Willie Randolph, who played 13 of his 18 major league seasons for Steinbrenner's club, recalled that even when the games meant nothing, they meant *everything* to King George.

"We played the Mayor's Trophy game for a bunch of years," Randolph told the *New York Times*. "I always looked forward to that. Steinbrenner got involved and tried to make it very serious. Like we had to win. It was do or die. That made it not so much fun. I remember feeling the pressure about winning: 'This is a big game. We're playing the Mets.'"

The big night arrived. Outside the stadium, Kenny Kramer, the eccentric real-life inspiration for the *Seinfeld* character, worked the crowd to drum up interest in his quixotic mayoral campaign. Inside, boosters for both teams exchanged chants and good-natured ribbing. The atmosphere was electric.

Roughly one third of those in attendance were there to cheer on the "visitors" from Queens, who arrived via bus ride over the Triborough Bridge with a police escort then erupted for three runs in the first inning—a development that shocked the other two-thirds. Mets starter Dave Mlicki, who'd won only two of his 13 previous starts, was masterful in striking out eight with a mix of curveballs and changeups. The Yankees threatened in the eighth

Through 2014, the Yankees led the Mets 56–42 (.571) in head-to-head regular season meetings.

A Mets fan in a sea of Yankees fans' stands during the Mets' three-run first inning on June 16, 1997. *(Andrew Savulich)*

when Paul O'Neill and Pat Kelly each singled with one out, but Mlicki regained control, closing out the inning by inducing Cecil Fielder to ground into a force-out and Tino Martinez to hit a routine fly ball to center. John Olerud, who doubled home the go-ahead run in the first inning, added a two-run single in the seventh. Final score: Mets 6, Yankees 0.

For one night, at least, the decades-old debate over which team was better could be settled with a simple point of the finger to the scoreboard. There was real power in that, for even when the Mets were world champs, someone would note that they hadn't reached the summit by knocking off the Yankees, as if that was the true measure of greatness. But there were no invisible asterisks on this night. On this night, New York belonged to the Mets.

The Yankees won the next two games, restoring order to George Steinbrenner's universe.

According to a 2014 Quinnipiac University poll, New York City baseball fans favor...

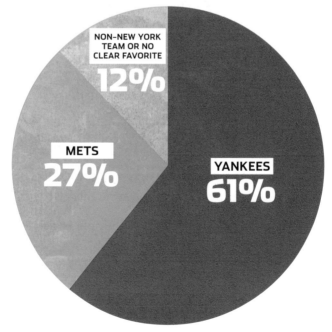

NON–NEW YORK TEAM OR NO CLEAR FAVORITE
12%

METS
27%

YANKEES
61%

42

Million Reasons You Can't Forget Bobby Bonilla

The Mets' decision in January 2000 to sever ties with disgruntled outfielder/first baseman Bobby Bonilla is one that they will be paying for until the year 2035.

A Bronx native, Bobby Bo rose to stardom with the Pittsburgh Pirates. From 1986 to 1991, he had a .284 batting average with 868 hits, 191 doubles, 114 home runs, and 500 RBI. He led the league in extra-base hits in 1990 and in doubles in 1991. He was also an All-Star four years in a row and a three-time Silver Slugger winner.

In 1991, Bonilla became a free agent. The Mets reeled him in with a five-year deal worth $29 million, making him the highest-paid player in baseball. But his production trailed off almost immediately and his abrasive personality didn't earn him many friends in and around the organization. In 1995, the Mets traded Bonilla and a player to be named later (minor leaguer Jimmy Williams) to the Baltimore Orioles for Damon Buford and Alex Ochoa.

After the surly slugger wore out his welcome in Baltimore, he moved on to the Florida Marlins (where he won a World Series) and then the Los Angeles Dodgers. In November 1998, the Dodgers traded Bonilla back to the Mets for reliever Mel Rojas. Again, his level of play did not measure up to expectations—the 36-year-old batted an atrocious .160 with four homers and 18 RBI in 60 games—and he clashed with manager Bobby Valentine over a lack of playing time.

His second stint in New York also included an infamous incident during Game 6 of the 1999 NLCS. While the Mets were fighting for their playoff lives in a game the Braves would win in 11 innings, Bonilla reportedly sat in the clubhouse playing cards with teammate Rickey Henderson.

After the season ended, the Mets got to work on ridding themselves of Bonilla for good. But the club still owed him $5.9 million for the next and final year of his bloated contract. The two sides struck a deal: a schedule of 25 deferred payments that wouldn't begin until 2011 but would run through 2035. Including eight percent compounded interest, the total cost to the Mets was projected to be $29.8 million. But a 2013 report by CBSSports.com revealed that Bonilla actually had *two* payment arrangements in place with the team. By the time they're paid off, the report stated, the total cost to the Mets will be $42 million.

That's an awful lot of money to pay someone to go away. But the Bonilla situation "was a distraction and a problem we needed to address this off-season," Mets GM Steve Phillips said in announcing the buyout. Bonilla was granted his release and signed with the Braves three weeks later.

 **DID YOU KNOW?** Before they agreed to pay Bobby Bonilla to disappear, the Mets negotiated a similar buyout with Bret Saberhagen, who pitched for the team from 1992 to 1995. For 25 years starting in 2004, Saberhagen receives annual deferred payments of $250,000.

That Bonilla's pact with the Mets will be paying him until he's old enough to collect Social Security has been held up as an example of front-office incompetence. On the plus side, by buying out Bonilla, the Mets freed up enough money in the short term to improve their rotation, acquiring Mike Hampton from the Astros. Without him, the Mets likely would not have won the 2000 NLCS. Then, when Hampton departed as a free agent, the team received a compensatory pick in the 2001 amateur draft, which it used to select David Wright.

Bobby Bonilla is among those major league players with at least:

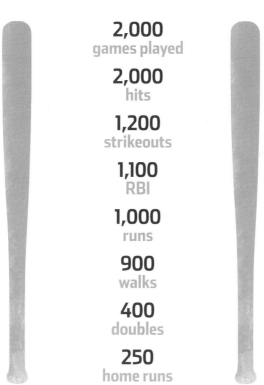

2,000
games played

2,000
hits

1,200
strikeouts

1,100
RBI

1,000
runs

900
walks

400
doubles

250
home runs

Sources

Bjarkman, Peter. *New York Mets Encyclopedia*. Sports Publishing, 2001.

Bock, Duncan and John Jordan. *The Complete Year-By-Year N.Y. Mets Fan's Almanac*. Three Rivers Press, 1992.

Breslin, Jimmy. *Can't Anybody Here Play This Game?* The Viking Press, 1963.

DeVito, Carlo. *Yogi: The Life & Times of an American Original*. Triumph Books, 2014.

Golenbock, Peter. *Amazin': The Miraculous History of New York's Most Beloved Baseball Team*. St. Martin's Press, 2002.

Klein, Frederick. *For the Love of the Mets*. Triumph Books, 2009.

Markusen, Bruce. *Tales from the New York Mets Dugout: A Collection of the Greatest Mets Stories Ever Told*. Sports Publishing, 2012.

Schoor, Gene. *Seaver*. Contemporary Books, 1986.

Silverman, Matthew. *Best Mets: Fifty Years of Highs and Lows from New York's Most Agonizingly Amazin' Team*. Rowman & Littlefield, 2014.

Silverman, Matthew. *New York Mets: The Complete Illustrated History*. MVP Books, 2011.

Newspapers and Magazines

Men's Journal

New York Daily News

New York Newsday

New York Times

The Saratogian

Wall Street Journal

Websites

BallparksofBaseball.com

Baseball-Almanac.com

Baseball-Reference.com

BaseballChronology.com

BillJamesOnline.com

Biography.com

ESPN.com

MLB.com

sabr.org (Society for American Baseball Research)

TheBaseballJournal.com

Acknowledgments

We would like to thank our friends at Triumph Publishing for coming up with this great concept and for giving us the opportunity to write one of the first books in the *Numbers Don't Lie* series. The fact that it was about the New York Mets was, for me, very gratifying. Our editor, Jesse Jordan, was great to work with. Under a tight deadline, he kept us on track but gave us the freedom to tell the story we wanted to tell.

Thanks, also, to our agent, Laurie Hawkins, for her ongoing support and encouragement.

Special thanks to longtime Mets fan and journalist Wayne Fish for his editorial support and to Mark Rosenman for connecting us with Mets alumni.

Mets fans live through the bad times and cherish the good times. Hopefully, you'll appreciate our efforts.

—Russ

I'd like to echo Russ' comments and also recognize the contributions of Eric "Sowah" Saranik (whose father made him leave Game 6 of the 1986 World Series at the top of the 10th inning to beat the traffic), my barber Phil Fichera, Adam Wolsky, and the immortal Chico Escuela.

—Adam